About The Author

Bryan M. Kuderna is a Certified Financial Planner™, Life Underwriter Training Council Fellow, Investment Adviser Representative and the founder of Kuderna Financial Team. He is a perennial qualifier for the financial industry's prestigious Million Dollar Round Table®. Bryan is a guest speaker nationwide at universities, teaching hospitals, government offices, and legal and accounting associations, on the subject of financial literacy. He holds a Bachelor of Science in Finance and Economics from The College of New Jersey. He has also studied at The University of Economics in Prague, Czech Republic and The University of Tampa. In his spare time, Bryan enjoys serving on The Community YMCA's Board of Directors, The Asbury Park Rotary Club, local economic development committees, and is a fellow of Lead New Jersey (Class of 2016). He has also completed the National Marathon in Washington, D.C. and an International Ironman in Mont Tremblant, Canada. He is a Millennial.

www.thewhitebook.net

Millennial Millionaire

A Guide to Become a Millionaire by 30

Bryan M. Kuderna, CFP®, LUTCF

The stories throughout this book are real. The associated names of clients, companies, and individuals have been changed to protect their privacy. Any historical or financial errors are the sole responsibility of the author. The author does not provide tax or legal advice, any matters of tax or law should be referred to a qualified attorney or accountant.

Table of Contents

Introduction

"A foolish faith in authority is the worst enemy of truth."
- Albert Einstein

I gazed through my dorm room window across the neatly manicured campus of The College of New Jersey, struggling to make a Half-Windsor knot out of my Dad's old tie. No matter how many times I tried, it looked like a clip-on that couldn't reach my belly button. I offset the funny looking tie with a wrinkled button-down shirt, corduroys that didn't match, and white tube socks. Having never thought of bringing a belt to college, I untucked the shirt just enough to cover my waistline. Time for one last check in the dusty mirror on my closet door, *damn I look good.*

Moments later, I was cruising along I-95, windows down, enjoying the spring air in route to our satellite office in Plainfield, NJ. I was bored of classwork and excited to start my internship. I wasn't too sure of this business I was entering, but I had some strange sort of confidence that this is what I would spend my life doing.

I arrived at a fancy office building with floor-to-ceiling windows and was directed by a secretary to the main conference room. We relaxed into leather executive seats at a long mahogany table filled with twelve new faces. There was a nervous energy that permeated the office. Someone whispered to me to lose the tie, we were supposed to be connecting to the "Working Man."

Across from me sat a very attractive lady wearing sexy attire that pushed the business casual limits. Wavy black hair trickled down in front of her shoulders, stopping just short of her well exposed chest. I quickly discovered the common knowledge that she was a stripper. Next to me sat a young man in a navy blue suit. His light brown hair stood straight up like an electrocuted cartoon character, he appeared to be a few years older than me (25 at the time). He kept fidgeting in his seat as the side conversations dimmed. I leaned forward to introduce myself, he casually slid his business card over the table to me, "Vice President", the card read.

Two guys stood at the front of the table ready to take charge, cocky and money hungry. Vinny was dressed in a tight baby blue Brooks Brothers sweater with extremely gelled hair; imagine the hair scene from Something About Mary combined with a punk on Jersey Shore. He was 26 at the time, but certainly looked like the youngest in the room. Vinny was single, but wore a gold plated wedding band in an attempt to present maturity. Next to him was the "seasoned veteran", Sam. Sam was 5'4" on his tippy toes, bald, and every bit Joe Pesci. He adorned a distant expression that feigned interest.

"Everyone listen up!" Vinny shouted in the deepest voice he could muster. We all stopped talking and gave him our attention. "How many of you read this?" He held up a copy of *Missed Fortune 101: A Starter Kit to Becoming a Millionaire*, like a preacher bestowing The Bible. No one raised their hand and Vinny went into enforcer mode, shouting F-bombs left and right at the group's laziness. The dissection of this book was interesting, albeit in a Napoleon dialogue strewn with curse words. Meanwhile the Joe Pesci lookalike sat silently in the corner, eyeing us like prey.

Vinny then completed an absurd financial sales presentation known as a "Turbo Engine Talk". The little bald guy stood up and moved to the easel, "You guys have all seen this talk and you know how to prospect. Let's see who's been doing their homework." Everyone in the room perked up with an added seriousness, as Sam was at least twice our age. My colleagues went around the table, explaining how many prospects they had seen, how many applications they had submitted, and how much money they were making. The Vice President, myself, and my fellow intern and soon to be partner, Jim, were automatically skipped. A few other advisors, all relatively new to the business and under the age of 24, quickly squeaked out a canned answer of how many folks they had met with and that "it's going rough but things are definitely getting better".

At the end of the table, sat a pretty girl with olive skin and dark eyes, wearing a grey single button blazer with matching pencil skirt. Her freshly pressed white shirt rounded out a nice conservative look. I noticed she avoided the small talk moments earlier and now appeared nervous to make her confession. "I submitted a couple of applications on some friends, but haven't closed any cases yet. I was at a wedding this past weekend; I know I could have pitched it to so many people but I didn't," she stammered as she looked down at the table. Sam and Vinny shook their heads and then offered a few words of encouragement. I still had no idea what these applications were that they were all so enamored with.

The whole meeting seemed to collapse when *Fat Jill* stood up to speak. I used to get upset when my coworkers threw this nickname around, but it was their way of separating her from our secretary, politely dubbed *MILF Jill*. Across from me sat a middle-aged woman who was, shall we say, "a bit rotund". She wore stained blue sweat pants and a faded green polo shirt with little holes on the sleeve. It wasn't that her appearance was not wealth management typical, but that an odor infused her surroundings which could literally knock you down. *Fat Jill's* short grey hair bounced side to side as she anxiously engaged the audience.

"Ok!" she shouted as she leaned into the table, "I've been having a damn good time prospecting." What came out of her mouth next almost changed the path of my career. "The target market I've been pounding are Churches. The other day I visited two church groups right in my town. The road coming up here had a whole buncha churches and you can be damn sure I'm gunna stop in everyone one of em on my way back." The tirade went on addressing how easy it was to get in these places and push her service.

I waited for Sam and Vinny to interject and suggest another avenue. "Do you guys see that?" Sam shouted, for the first time showing animation. "Do you see that enthusiasm!? That's what the rest of you are lacking. That kind of enthusiasm and prospecting is what makes us money!"

Jim and I turned to each other to make eye contact. *Dude, where the hell are we right now?!*

After two hours of ranting and raving by these so-called mentors who sounded like they had chugged ten cans of Red Bull, Sam and Vinny concluded the meeting. I just witnessed a reenactment of that famous Boiler Room scene in which Ben Affleck pumps up his rookie brokers.

"All right that's it, book some freaking turbo talks and we'll handle the rest. Now you two, Jim and Bryan, you guys stay." They kindly imparted some professional advice on us. Vinny explained that a career in financial planning was like water in a bath tub, every day you smack the water and little waves ripple back and forth long after you've left. He said that at least one night a week we'd go home so stressed that we'd want to beat our girlfriends, but he beseeched us to keep the water level and not let the waves continue to ripple. *Beautifully worded advice sensei.*

This room of upstanding citizens were to be my comrades. These insane mentors would be my guides into the industry, the fiduciaries who would actually be handling my clients. This 25 year-old Vice President would be my manager, who would monitor my progress and pave the way for my growth.

As fate would have it, my new coworkers would all eventually leave the agency, some like the stripper on their own accord, others for lack of production, and a select few by force. The lovely *Fat Jill* exited in handcuffs for stealing a sizeable check from her partner (we later learned that she was living out of her minivan while working for us). Another colleague of mine was not fired, but actually disappeared overnight. After a lengthy investigation, authorities determined that he fled the country after embezzling $2 million dollars of his clients' money (he's still missing). The miniature mentors would also be fired within a couple of years, a result of countless customer complaints and an illegal practice known as "churning" and "twisting".

Unfortunately, this did not happen until after sparking huge riffs between my family and close friends, and stealing my money by whiting out commission splits on my clients' contracts! I was unknowingly earning 20% of commissions on my clients while they took 80%.

So began my career as a Financial Advisor with one of the largest institutions in the world, granted at an office temporarily abandoned by upper management. A career in which I would witness first-hand the good, the bad, and the extremely ugly. I can say without hesitation, I would not trade it for the world.

Step 1: The Future is Yours

"The future ain't what it used to be."
- Yogi Berra

If you want to become a millionaire by your thirtieth birthday, you must first understand where we are headed. There are hundreds of biographies on world leaders in finance and economics at your local library. However you may notice a few similarities from the pictures of the author on the inside cover... they are mostly white, typically college educated, usually lacking financial designations, and OLD. Today's financial pundits are male, stale, and pale.

These people aren't speaking to us! They have great ideas, they publicize all the mistakes and coulda shoulda woulda's of the last bubble, but few if any confer what's next.

The truth is that no one is really reaching millennials. From K-12 you probably learned about Biology, Algebra, American Literature, Chemistry, and Gym, everything except for business. I meet on a regular basis with doctors, engineers, scientists, even Ivy League grads, so many of whom don't yet know how to balance a checkbook, interpret their FICO Score, or differentiate between credit card debt and student loan debt. To be honest, most of us graduating business school learned some incredible economic theory and crazy equations, but leave puzzled by such everyday fundamentals. A genius without education is like gold still buried in the mine. Tomorrow's geniuses need financial education!

To make things worse, America is a country that does not like to save anymore. From a micro standpoint, in 2006 amidst the height of the market, the annual household savings rate in America averaged -1.7%[1]. That's a minus sign right there! On a macro level, our country is ensnared in a web of debt exceeding $19,000,000,000,000[2]. What ever happened to Grandma and Grandpa telling us, "Son, you don't spend what you don't have." In Proverbs 22:6, Solomon encourages parents to, "Train up a child in the way he should go, and when he is old he will not depart from it." When you couple a lack of early education with bad habits it is a recipe for disaster.

In spite of the lack of formal schooling for financial literacy, the trend towards young professionals entering the financial advising field is promising. The US Bureau of Labor Statistics points out that "employment of financial advisors is expected to increase 30% from 2014-2024, far more than average. The primary influence is ageing… Baby Boomers needing retirement advice amidst decreasing pensions." The study clarifies the job prospects as – Financial Advisors attracted by high wages and few education requirements (more on this later). To add to that, of the 300,000+ Financial Advisors, less than 5% are currently under the age of thirty.[3]

As we go through this book and I share my stories and bits of wisdom, some from old farts and others from college kids, you'll notice that most subject matter isn't new or revolutionary. It's ever-tempting to reinvent the wheel, but like any science, it's not so much about discoveries as it is rediscoveries. Ben Franklin once said concerning his famous

---

[1] The Commerce Department- 2006
[2] USgovernmentdebt.org
[3] US Bureau of Labor Statistics, Personal Financial Advisors- 2015

almanac, "They contained the wisdom of many ages and nations... not a tenth part of the wisdom was my own."

History is also relayed in our own narrative. Watch a movie twice or reread a book, each time it seems to resonate differently. As life goes on and you succeed and fail, this editorial will surely teach different lessons. We will begin a journey by uncovering our passions in the transformative college years, then we'll progress through life by finding a happy job and eventually retiring, all with contributing hurdles and boosts to financial independence. Heed the advice herein and the eggs we crack will make you a delicious omelet; ignore these realities and your kitchen will be left a mess.

Step 2: Why Did You Go to College?

"The great aim of education is not knowledge, but action."
-Herbert Spencer

In my first few days as a student at The University of Tampa, I was blown away by the freedom, beautiful weather, and roughly 50:1 Female to Male ratio. I loved every minute of freshman year, but I would be completely lying if I said I had any clue as to why I was there or what I was trying to accomplish. Most current undergrads share a similar conundrum.

I later transferred to The College of New Jersey and received some excellent tips at orientation. TCNJ had hired a new Dean that year; he was some ex-Wall Street guy who supposedly killed it. He paced back and forth in front of the huge auditorium with an aura of confidence earned through years of brokering high stakes business deals combined with a dull realization that his audience were simply kids. We struggled through muggy heat to keep our eyes open from Tipsy Tuesday.

"Look I'm going to tell you guys the way it is... college is an incredible experience in which you'll dive into your classwork and be pushed hard to make the grade. But the truth of the matter is, later in your career you'll remember little if anything of the coursework that you were taught. However, what you'll never forget are the soft skills you're going to pick up along the way." Oh by the way, those "soft skills" come with an average price tag of $44,750 per year (private college)[4].

---

[4] Trends in College Pricing, College Board

He went on to say that of all the recruiters they dealt with, the number one fault and coincidentally most important trait they looked for, was communication. Fans of The Carnegie Institute will agree with this hypothesis, asserting that "15% of financial success is due to technical knowledge, the other 85% is to human engineering... Personality."[5] The orientation focused on honing this skill. *Wait, so you mean that funny, energetic waiter we had Friday night might be smarter than the 4.0 lab rat I'm next to in Trigonometry 201?* Guess it all depends on the metrics.

Our introductory talk concluded with the Dean telling us how the last surefire recommendations were to get an internship and study abroad. "Studying abroad is one of the greatest experiences you can ever allow yourself. Yah, you'll probably miss half of your classes to go to some coffee shop with the girl from Italy, but that's life." I don't know why but that statement seemed to etch itself into my memory, he spoke those words in a haze as if it were a real life experience just yesterday.

It's true that academics focus primarily on what is measurable, but not necessarily what is meaningful. Maybe this is what Einstein meant by saying that, "Imagination is more important than knowledge."

So do PHD's and enormous books on economic theorem help in this regard?

One of the starting points for America's financial troubles begins here on the perfectly landscaped and never-ending construction sites known as college campuses. The

---

[5] Carnegie Institute of Technology

Bachelor's Degree has now become the equivalent of Mom and Dad's High School Diploma.

If you think college is expensive now, wait until it's *your* kid's turn for higher education. According to BLS, Consumer Price Index, since 1983 the cost of a car has increased 44%. The cost for a tank of gas: 192%. What about the hyperinflation we'll soon discuss associated with Medical Care: 330%. Last but not least, college tuition has increased by 688% since 1983. As the single fastest-growing household expense, the projected cost for a baby born in 2013 to obtain a four-year college education at a private university is $424,425[6]!

That monster price tag does not even account for what has become the new norm, The Five-Year Plan. I was proud to achieve my degree in four years, in spite of attending four different colleges. Older folks probably wonder why that's special, as the typical undergraduate program is scheduled for four years. Well clearly they haven't met the "Super Senior", an additional year promoted by guidance counselors for a more thorough and less stressful experience. Does this have anything to do with the trillion dollar business and ultra-competitive college rating agencies? Nothing like teaching kids right out the gates to trade a sense of urgency for some delayed success. *But heck, one more year of frat parties and daytime naps, count me in!*

Often graduates will take it a step further, separating themselves from the pack by moving immediately on to a Master's program (26% of graduates go to Graduate School within one year[7]). As my bombastic Accounting 101 professor

---

[6] The College Board, 2013 Trends in College Pricing
[7] U.S. News- 2014

at Tampa used to scream at us, "Get a job and some experience dammit! The manager at my local Dunkin Donuts has an MBA!"

While college education plays an enormous role in society's development, it's not necessarily for everyone. "The Millionaire Next Door" effectively points out that there is actually a negative correlation between grad degrees and high accumulators of wealth. Most millionaires were business owners, and most of these business owners listed some or no post-secondary education. That includes icons of history- Thomas Edison admitted to only three months of formal education, and Henry Ford built an empire with less than a 6th grade education![8]

Today, the cost for one more year of college can easily eclipse $50,000 in tuition, room, and board (Sarah Lawrence costs $50,780 for tuition alone in 2014![9]). That far exceeds the income recent graduates average, immediately setting them back at least two years.

On the other side of this financial argument, please note that a century ago fewer than one in twenty Americans ever took a college *course*. And six decades ago minorities were not even allowed on many college grounds. Today society promotes college as an absolute for everyone, and even pay to entice minority students (and illegal immigrants) via affirmative action. Less than a decade ago the same leaders said every American should own a home, we saw the real estate epidemic those good intentions spawned. Might history repeat itself in another form?

---

[8] The Millionaire Next Door (1996)- Thomas Stanley, William Danko
[9] "Annual Survey of Colleges- 2014"- The College Board

I'll be the first to say that I love Obamacare's allowance for children under age 26 to stay on their parents' healthcare plans (full disclosure I took advantage of this benefit while starting this book). However, like the rest of the entitlements that plague our country, this lunch isn't free. Not only is it not free, it's yet another incentive to forgive my fellow youth from rushing into the work force. Once you giveth, you cannot taketh.

The other beef with college today, similar to high school… they are teaching the wrong subjects. Time Magazine ran an interesting article, *College Costs: Would Tuition Discounts Get More Students to Major in Science?*, which spurred then Governor Rick Scott of Florida to propose freezing tuition rates on *strategic areas* such as engineering, science, health care, and technology, while letting the costs of humanities and other majors rise. These *strategic areas* are not *soft skills*, these ones are not supposed to be forgotten upon graduation. A classroom may be a great simulator for the sciences, but reading a boring textbook usually doesn't help you sell the whale client.

So how does all this affect our country as a whole? Currently there are well over $1.2 trillion of outstanding student loans, a number that has tripled in the last decade. The Federal Reserve reports that 93% of all student loans are through the federal government. These are loans that do not require any underwriting. Of the waves of teenagers who enter college, more than two-thirds of them are getting by with student loans[10]. This is a rare debt in which lenders require no collateral (other than your hopeful future success), and after personally

---

[10] U.S. Department of Education

interviewing many college admissions counselors, I still have never heard of an actual limit on loans available.

Speaking of debt, did you get carried away with the shopping at Macy's last month? Overextend yourself by getting the new Lexus instead of last year's model? Rack up some huge debts on the blackjack tables? Don't' worry, a bankruptcy proceeding can wipe this slate clean. But what's that, you went to one of the top private colleges in your state to study biomedical engineering and were unable to find a job right out of college, thus falling far behind on your massive unsubsidized student loans? Sorry, no bankruptcy here (Bankruptcy Abuse Prevention and Consumer Protection Act of 2005), they're a shadow you can't outrun.

I recently met with a client of mine, a successful 32 year-old criminal attorney in New York City. He summarized the national phenomena perfectly by passionately impersonating a famous Goodfellas scene right in our office... "But now the guy's gotta come up with Paulie's money every week, no matter what. Business bad- f*** you pay me! Oh you had a fire- f*** you pay me! Place got hit by lightning huh- f*** you pay me!" I couldn't stop laughing at his comparison of mob boss, Paulie, and that "extortioner" Sallie Mae. The scariest part... we are a country that lives on plastic, we love credit cards as much as baseball. Even so, today there's more outstanding student loan debt than credit card debt[11]!

Higher education is still the key to a brighter future. However, the realities cannot afford to be ignored any longer. Academicians should embrace the idea of community college, online instruction, trade school, entrepreneurism and rally

---

[11] Federal Reserve Bank of New York- 2014

around the issue at hand. This should be a collaborative effort with a student-centric approach, not a pissing contest of new institutions versus old.

***

Let me share with you one of the saddest stories of my career, a collision of poor financial planning and American's educational system. In 2012 a good friend of mine and fellow board member at The YMCA gave me a call. "Hey Bry, I know this one won't be your ideal client, but she's a friend of the family and we'd really appreciate your help." Nick was a regional manager for a blossoming community bank. His referral was a lady named Jackie.

Jackie happens to be one of the nicest people I've ever met. She is an administrative assistant for an early developmental school for children. She works long hours for near minimum wage, and even picks up weekend shifts to make ends meet. I was introduced to her only months after she lost her husband to cancer. Rather than feeling sorry for herself, she did everything in her power to get her daughter through college while taking extra care inheriting the role of breadwinner.

Jackie's husband practiced the right habits I preach every day of paying yourself first, but he clearly did not have the professional counsel they deserved. He spent his career plowing money only into his company 401(k)'s, taking advantage of the tax deduction his accountant so craved. Throughout his working years, Mr. Anderson maintained a small amount of Group Term Life Insurance. As he got sicker, lost his job, and income dropped, this valuable insurance disappeared. Upon his passing, Jackie received $220,000 in her husband's

401(k) and a laughable death benefit from Social Security (today if a widow applies within two years of death of her spouse, and meets certain requirements, she may be entitled to a $255 lump sum death benefit)[12].

While Mr. Anderson's health deteriorated, so did the condition of their neglected home. Merge this with mounting health bills, limited work hours, and a child heading to college and you had a real pickle. When I met Jackie, she realized this $220,000 401(k) would not only have to get her daughter through college, pay off outstanding debts, and repair the house, but also last her lifetime. The harshest reality of the 401(k) was that every dollar that would come out would be taxed as ordinary income, for a household no longer able to file jointly. A brilliant young woman, her daughter Samantha NEEDED financial aid more than anyone I've met. However, being poor but not poor enough, white, and a US citizen, the odds were not in her favor. One would think that a single mom on a minimum salary would satisfy FAFSA (Free Application for Federal Student Aid), but remember that she needed that retirement money to live. Each distribution showed up as ordinary income and boosted her reportable income that much higher. The 401(k) was literally acting like a morphine drip to a dying patient.

Luckily, we were able to qualify her for a small Home Equity Line of Credit (HELOC) that could provide some much needed tax-free income and escape the evil eyes of FAFSA.

College is not cheap, and the costs only seem to be rising. So before your daughter goes to NYU because that's where her boyfriend is going, schedule a serious sit-down

---

[12] Socialsecurity.gov

regarding the pros and cons of this investment. If that six figure piece of paper is a goal for your children, then please plan accordingly. Let Jackie's story be a lesson to the lack of diversification outside of Qualified Plans such as the 401(k), and more importantly the abandonment of one of finance's most valuable tools, Life Insurance.

In 1935 the Daily featured an article titled, "Senior Men Face Life With Debts, Few Jobs", citing the average debt held by graduates at $200, with the tab for a four-year college eclipsing $2,000[13]. You be the judge on what has changed, or hasn't.

---

[13] "Senior Men Face Life With Debts, Few Jobs"- The Daily, 1935

Step 3: Stop Asking for Handouts

*"The worst thing you can do for those you love is the
things they could do for themselves."*
- President Abraham Lincoln

It's human nature to believe in cause and effect. Hundreds of thousands of young men and women graduate from prominent colleges every year, proudly carrying a new diploma, filled with a belief that now they must be owed something. Universities spend obscene amounts of money marketing a neatly packaged product that alumni will get what's coming just by obtaining their degree. However, studying all those years to then become a rookie is a tough realization. Everyone remembers how John Wooden won ten national championships in twelve seasons, but few realize that he coached the famed UCLA Bruins for fifteen years before putting on a ring. It is not supposed to be easy starting out.

My wakeup call came the summer after I graduated TCNJ. In a last ditch effort to escape my moronic mentors from scamming everyone we knew, one of my associates introduced me to his cousin Ron, who also happened to be our top producer (with merely a high school education). I met this Tony Soprano look alike with my partner Jim at 7:00 AM one morning to pick his brain. He gave us a few pointers and said he was onboard to tutor or do joint work with us. In his tough Bayonne accent he left us with some parting words I never forgot, "Listen to me, if you want to even have a chance in this business, you've got to be ready to put in ten hour days, everyday... and don't expect any pat on the back." There went my long lunches and midday naps.

Me, myself, and I would be directly accountable for every dollar of income produced. This was a frightening reality that shortcuts weren't allowed, and crutches would not be provided. Tis the life of an entrepreneur, but also a life all young adults will face in coming years of self-reliant fiscal stability.

As our country, the greatest nation known to mankind, unfolds a balance sheet of devastating proportions, it's imperative we detect the problem. The greatest trouble is one of expectation, or rather entitlement.

At the home level, young professionals are living in Mom and Dad's basement longer than ever. Everyone has heard the story of parents walking two miles to school every day, uphill both ways. After that they eventually turned eighteen and were booted out of the house, "You're on your own, now find a job and pay rent!"

Today there is a trend politely termed "Delayed Onset Adulthood" or more commonly, "Boomerang Kids". They go to college for four to six years, spend around $150k on education, only to end up back home searching for a job. Then fall back into a comfort zone of home cooked food, no bills, and soon celebrate their thirtieth birthday in the same old backyard. This book aims for you to turn thirty as a millionaire, not Mom and Dad's tenant.

Humans are creatures of habit. When one grows up watching Grandparents enjoying their golden years and parents preparing for them, it's natural to follow suit with comparable expectations. The scary reality of it is this... the way in which we millennials retire will be entirely different than what we've witnessed thus far. Once we get past the basis that graduation doesn't *give* us a job, we must then grasp that landing a job doesn't *give* us a retirement.

Social Security, Pensions, Medicaid, Welfare, Obamacare, etc. all come at a cost. As society trades in these autopilot programs for a do-it-yourself approach, the responsibility to earn, save, and plan falls on the individual. Never has it been more important to start early; but unfortunately incomes are starting later than ever.

Those autopilot programs are the source of constant political debate. The Heritage Foundation cited that in 2014, 66% of the government's budget went to entitlement programs[14]. Politicians on both sides of the aisle are accustomed to going in the backyard to pick from the money tree. The money tree can do amazing things and it's such a beautiful plant. But that money tree is awfully expensive to water!

Have you ever heard the term Ponzi Scheme? It is defined by Merriam-Webster as "an investment swindle in which some early investors are paid off with money put up by later ones in order to encourage more and bigger risks." This term comes from the swindler Charles Ponzi who would sell discounted postal reply coupons bought abroad and redeemed in the US.

You probably know the name Bernie Madoff, the architect of the most famous and largest Ponzi Scheme in recent history. In short, he would take large investments from the wealthy (and gullible) and promise extraordinary returns. In the following year a new wave of funds would come ashore by

---

[14] www.heritage.org – 2014 Federal Spending Charts

more investors, a portion of this new money was then paid out to the original investors in the form of a dividend. These repayments to investors consistently outperformed the overall market by gross margins. The only caveat of course, they weren't getting their money and growth back, they were getting some other suckers' money.

Madoff's was the largest in *recent* history, but the largest in *history* is housed by our own federal government... Social Security. People think a down market or poor stock returns seen on TV may account for the current funding crisis. This actually isn't accurate as Social Security funds are invested in government securities. Well then, is it inflation paired with historically low interest rates creating this disastrous mosaic? Perhaps a contributing factor, but still not the underlying problem. The bottom line is the demographics don't add up. Waves of baby boomers are retiring and they simply aren't being replaced quickly enough (see thirty-year old in basement). On top of that, our ancestors who collected in the 1940's and 1950's for five years of retirement didn't pull from the pot as long as our nursing home parents do for 25-35 years.

Social Security is the cornerstone of retirement today, accounting for 40% of the average retiree's income[15]. Because of its overwhelming dependence, discussing Social Security reform has been considered taboo by politicians. Grab a hold of it and your toast. However, even the Social Security Administration admits concerns...

Let's start in 1930 for a brief history. Reports show that approximately one in ten people were covered by some form of defined benefit pension. Our saving grace, Social Security, did

---

[15] U.S. News- 2014

not even exist yet. That bears repeating, the most relied upon
and debated fund in America today, did not exist for our first
154 years.

Social Security started in 1935 as OASI (Old Age and
Survivors Insurance), a pay-as-you-go-system signed by
President Franklin Delano Roosevelt. In 1935 there were over
forty workers per beneficiary[16]. Five years later, benefits began
being paid in 1940. Fun Fact: the first beneficiary was Ida May
Fuller who received a monthly check of $22.54, she lived to be
100!

Fast forward and as employment demographics shifted,
Congress took action in 1983. Amendments were passed that
increased the Normal Retirement Age (NRA) from 65 to 67 as
well as introducing income taxation on Social Security Benefits.
The major amendments enacted in 1983 were exemplified in
that year's annual trustees' report, which mentioned "actuarial
balance" for another 75 years, but allowing for increasing
income tax and other measures to keep the system balanced.
Their high cost projection, recognized as Alternative III, actually
showed exhaustion of OASI and Disability Insurance (DI) trust
funds as early as 2027. Even then congress was planning for
failure.

A decade later, Congress acted to reallocate payroll tax
earmarked for OASI to the Disability Insurance program, as
figures for the DI trust fund were (and are) even worse than our
retirement platform.

How did that all pan out? The Social Security
Administration's 2009 Annual Trustees Report quoted, "Benefits

---

[16] OASDI Trustees Report- 2012, Table IV.B2

are expected to be paid in full until 2037, when the trust fund reserves are expected to be exhausted."[17]

Today there are roughly two workers per beneficiary. Now we have just two horses trying to drag a train in excess of thirty years instead of what started as forty horses pulling a cart for only two years. Were those old green statements we used to gawk at every year really eliminated to "Go Green" and to save the country a few cents on postage... or so most of us would slowly start forgetting that program is even there?

President George H.W. Bush called the collapse of Social Security reform one of the greatest disappointments of his presidency, again kicking the problem down the road to the next generation.

A mirror image of Social Security can be observed in modern day pensions, the second largest source of retiree income. My home state of New Jersey currently has over $40 billion of unfunded pension liabilities (not to mention at least $51 billion of healthcare unfunded liabilities)[18]. Governor Chris Christie has become national news, not because he's skipping contributions to the state pension fund (which several of his predecessors on both sides of the aisle already have done), but because he's actually spotlighting the problem.

Today pensions are close to extinct, and retirement can last as long as our career if not longer. Therein lies the frustration towards school and law enforcement unions, who may reflexively complain about a slightly larger payroll

---

[17] OASDI Trustees Report- 2009
[18] NJ Spotlight- Why NJ's Unfunded Liability for Retirees is $90 billion and Rising

deduction towards their pension fund. Let's do a quick exercise to compare their retirement to the rest of America in the private sector... Most economists today recommend that one spends down his or her portfolio at a rate of 4-5% per year throughout retirement. That means that if you were proactive enough to accumulate $1,000,000 in your 401(k) upon retirement, you should be able to generate $40,000-$50,000 of annual income for the rest of your life. How many common folks or small business owners do you know with seven figures in their Individual Retirement Account (IRA) or brokerage account? Not many. But how many cops and teachers do you know who grieve over the Cost of Living Adjustment being reduced on their $70,000 lifetime pension?

We Americans have adopted the habit of entering the workforce at a much later age, retiring at a younger age, and living to a much older age. We can debate it as a problem or an opportunity, but we must agree it's a shift to personal responsibility that demands aggressive saving sooner than ever.

***

Retiring after a life of hard work and asking for a boost is one thing. Being young and healthy with your hand out is a whole other animal. Nothing is more infuriating than seeing the people who have learned how to "beat the system". While many of us laugh at the lady on line at 7-11 with food stamps in one hand and the latest smartphone in the other, this is a serious issue to be addressed.

The ultimate gift, where maybe the greatest disparity between income and benefits rests, is in welfare. Some forms of welfare, such as unemployment, provide an individual temporary assistance when they're down and out. But a reduced check and shortened benefit period are clear incentives to get back in the work force. That's why extending these benefits further and further every year is not rational. Being out of work is bad, there should be no reward for it... just enough to get you by when life happens.

There are other welfare systems that throw economic theory and the concept of incentives right out the window. Take food stamps for instance, the USDA reported that 20% of American households were on food stamps in 2013. SNAP (Supplemental Nutrition Assistance Program) provides for 23 million households, an increase of 51% from 2009. In 2013 SNAP cost American taxpayers $79,641,880,000[19]. If you don't get a job, you can spend your life on food stamps. We'll save politics for later, but this is one of President Obama's proudest accomplishments, and one of the Republican's biggest frustrations.

I was catching up with my friend, Don, recently at a fancy gala. He's an extremely motivated volunteer, and the proud director of a local Boys and Girls Club. I asked how the club was doing amidst a downturn in donations and an overall tough climate for nonprofits.

In his customary optimistic approach, Don touted what an impact the club was having on the underprivileged, rattling off story after story of kids staying off the streets and doing homework or playing sports. After a couple of cocktails he seemed to open up a bit and as sadly said, "You know what really bothers me at the club? So we charge $20 annually for a membership, an attempt to get the parents committed to the club as much as the kids. Unfortunately, more and more of the

---

[19] USDA.gov – SNAP Monthly Data

parents are sending their children to the club and refuse to pay the $20. In an effort to not be inconsiderate, we politely compromised and asked them to send their child to class with $1 for a daily pass, an accommodating finance plan for the $20 dues. Instead, the parents balked at the $1 charge screaming Bloody Mary."

As a board they refused to cave and agreed that allowing parents to forego any payment was only going to perpetuate this entitlement problem by setting the example to their kids that if you hold out long enough, you'll get what you want anyways. Resembling the broken window theory, we see one broken window and think that is the norm, one small expression allows us to think what else can we get away with?

Why do these entitlements equate to the perfect storm? Our parents had the fortuitous ability to overlook financial planning with the assurance that The Man (big company) and The Government (Social Security/Welfare) would take care of them someday. Today's youngsters may not be so fortunate, and we are still dragging our feet on financial literacy.

So should we blame us mere individuals for digging this hole? Are we getting this stamp of spending approval from our neighbors?

What about all the banks bailed out in 2008? After awful business decisions and careers of excess, they were all deemed Too Big To Fail by our own government. This financial theory of moral hazard, the ability to take undue risks with the confidence that potential losses will be borne by others, spread like wildfire across Wall Street. If the biggest and brightest of the financial industry are told it's ok not to plan and live high on the hog, what is Joe Schmo supposed to think?

The baby boomers have nearly bankrupted our country on an American credit card; will China and other investors extend our credit line further? The next generation shouldn't be required to carry the whole burden, nor are we permitted to put down our share.

My parents used to always tell me that "Nothing in this house is given; only earned." Mark Twain said it a little differently, "Don't go around saying the world owes you a living. The world owes you nothing. It was here first." So please don't rely on the handouts, but rather proudly pave your own way with the steps recommended herein.

Step 4: Ignore The Jones'

"In the case of natural desires few people go wrong and only in one way, in the direction of too much."
- Aristotle: Ethics

College may be made up of sleepless nights, cloudy memories of early morning clubbing, and war stories over Ramen Noodles, but once you leave those lovely dorm halls and graduate into the real world, the Jones' will introduce themselves. A champagne taste develops on an old beer budget.

People feel an innate ability to always have to keep up. Children are raised to compete and be better than the next kid. Sadly, as adults one of the most commonly used measuring sticks is money. How do you tell if one has money? In today's world, unless you have a tax return or bank account statements, it's not easy. With financing provided for apparently anything under the sun, anyone can get that dream home or fancy car.

The most exasperating part of being a financial planner, bar none, is confronting people on this issue. "But Bryan, there's just no money left at the end of the month. We want to save money for Timmy and Johnny so they can go to college, except it's not possible!"

"Well Mr. and Mrs. Flash, it's possible, but Timmy and Johnny's college fund is sitting out front in the driveway." Notice the brand new Lexus, BMW, and weekend Hummer tricked out with rims and TV's in the headrest so the little ones can watch SpongeBob. Swallow your ego and save your kids.

The Chinese said a thousand years ago, "He who treads softly goes far". You do not need to blow your annual bonus to put a sign on your chest that says I have some money too.

Let me tell you of an elderly couple I was referred to early in my career during 2010. Mrs. Jones never worked, a sweet lady who enjoyed life as a homemaker. Mr. Jones was a truck driver, who eventually went out on total "disability" and collects one helluva pension. They live in a beautiful upscale neighborhood, directly across the street from his cardiologist. The only difference is the cardiologist pays his mortgage; my clients did not and were way underwater. Mrs. Jones drives a Mercedes and Mr. Jones a BMW, both new leases. In spite of their six figure income from an incredible disability benefit through the union, and collecting on social security, they managed to also rack up $85,000 of credit card debt on seven different cards. The average interest rate on those cards was around 22%.

With no way to climb out of this hole, they humbly declared bankruptcy. I hated to see this happen, but maybe it was the medicine they needed. Nope. Not even one year after their bankruptcy I received a call from Mr. Jones because the fella at the dealership offered him a great deal on the new model of the Mercedes convertible. Despite my abrupt warnings, Mr. Jones proceeded to take a loan against his only remaining asset, Cash Value inside his Whole Life Insurance policy, to buy this beauty. Mr. and Mrs. Jones- excellence that feels it has to be proclaimed, by the mere fact of its proclamation admits the doubt of its existence. Jesus imparted similar counsel in Luke 14:11, "For everyone who exalts himself will be humbled, and he who humbles himself will be exalted."

Rich people often don't look like we think they would. Surveys show that most millionaires in the USA are first generation (about 80% according to the Cato Institute)[20]. Meaning that the longer a family is here in the states, the more they adapt to our consumption lifestyle and so the money goes. Poor people seem to be more driven by a need to impress reference groups rather than their own wellbeing.

I love to go to Atlantic City and blow a little cash, emphasis on little. Now I make a pretty decent living, but sometimes fall prey to visions of one day being a "high roller". They toss the chips around and order the Pina Coladas next to the girl with fake boobs. Believe it or not that "high roller" usually is *not* rich, but is actually skating by and gambling his savings account. Another sap lured in by American media of flash and pizzazz, not targeted at the wealthy, but the weak. Now that's called Product Placement.

Society has taken the liberty of redefining what's necessary. The luxuries our parents or grandparents once splurged on are now considered the status quo. If your daughter doesn't have the latest Coach or Louis Vuitton bag, she's not cool. If your son is wearing Reebok's and not the latest Jordan's, he may not jump as high.

Take a look at shopping trends. Bargain stores such as Sears and K-Mart were stalwarts for generations of Americans. Today they are disintegrating. If you are able to find one, you'll notice an eerie feel of a ghost town and the few shoppers present are usually senior citizens enjoying the open space to walk for exercise. In place of these great deals, there are flourishing luxury malls. In spite of the economic downturn,

---

[20] www.cato.org- 2011

these locations are popping up everywhere from major cities to suburbia. People once wanted, now they *need* the opportunity to relax in a leather recliner with a Chi Latte and browse handbags often marked up 300% or perhaps sunglasses marked up 1,000% over wholesale (source: Kadet).

To take shopping statistics a step further, we are now a society that enjoys shopping for not only accessories, but also body parts! The American Society of Plastic Surgery reports that Tummy Tuck procedures are up 86% since 2000. 2012 was a record year for the business with 14.6 million cosmetic procedures. The number one most common procedure, you guessed it... boobs[21].

So have we become a nation of peacocks, completely obsessed with conspicuous consumption? The statistics may say so. If you're thinking of joining the party and wasting your bonus check on some crap you can show off, perhaps you'll want to read a recent study by The Harris Poll. These pollsters showed that the majority of women think a man in a fancy car is compensating for "shortcomings".

---

[21] www.plasticsurgery.org

Step 5: The Million Dollar Phone

*"He who sows sparingly shall reap sparingly. He who
sows generously shall reap generously."*
- Paul to The Corinthians, The Bible

We sat in an old run down Bed and Breakfast in the heart of Asbury Park, the smell of the ocean wafting through the air. There were antiques littered everywhere in this aged Victorian. The walls were a pastel yellow with scattered paintings that could have been worth $20 or $20,000. My business partner, Jim, and I looked on with bewilderment at this menagerie of ten middle aged entrepreneurs being entertained by a man I swore was a crackhead. We both thought we had the wrong location as this circle of chairs really felt like an AA meeting.

Nope, we were at the right location. This "networking event" was a meet and greet for those wanting to become skilled at social media.

"I've got almost a thousand followers!" the crackhead screamed. He was tall, sickly skinny, with tight knit cornrows, a raggedy T-shirt, and baggy torn jeans. His eyes looked like silver dollars as he spoke faster than Bhusta Rhymes in his prime. "The key is in me tweeting and following as many people as possible." I was familiar with Facebook from college, but this Twitter site had recently come out and I had no idea what he was talking about. So on and on he went flailing his arms and bragging how no one would ever get as many followers as him. The other people in our circle were captivated and continued to ask questions. The part that really cracked me up (no pun intended) was that our ringleader here was currently unemployed.

Jim and I stared at our watches waiting for the right time to make an impromptu exit. After an hour of idiom we politely excused ourselves.

This is how I began my business, and it is the fastest route to becoming a millionaire by thirty. A rich person's currency is not money, but rather relationships. Social capital is what makes your iPhone worth $300 and a CEO's worth $1 million. As the shy kid in high school, these gatherings taught invaluable lessons. What we fear most is usually what we need to do. For the rest of my generation who are graduating from excellent colleges with enormous debt and record low employment for pre-thirties, this is how we must start our careers. Pretend the entitlements don't exist, forget the Jones', and get straight to building your network.

As the globalization in mass communication becomes consuming, we must revert back to personal contacts to gain a competitive advantage. Social media has done a world of good and reconnected many a lost friend, but it's also taking away our natural ability to communicate with people. *Remember from Chapter one, according to recruiters communication is the most important yet lacking skill today.* I find myself talking more with my friends through e-mails and texts than in person.

A perfect example of this revolution is online dating. There was a time when if you couldn't pick up a chick at the bar or woo the cute girl at work, you were out of luck and had better step up your game. A publishing in *Proceedings of the National Academy of Sciences* by John Cacioppo found that 35%

of new marriages start online, and 45% of couples met online[22].
Are we not the generation infatuated with all things organic?
Nothing wrong with this new development, but what's organic
in half of all relationships starting out like shopping for a car on
www.autotrader.com?

Mankind has traded the shared knowledge we get from
unique relationships for the mass data spewed out by robots.
Herbert Simon (Nobel Prize in Economics) famously posited that
a wealth of information creates a poverty of attention, spurring
the need to allocate attention efficiently. It's as if we're trying
to sip information from a fire hose. Take this for instance, every
60 minutes there are over 6,000 hours of YouTube videos
uploaded. Such saturation isn't just in the new age internet... in
1976 supermarkets stocked approximately 9,000 items at a
time, today they stock in excess of 40,000 items (mind you we
each regularly use only 150 of them, on average)[23]. People are
inundated with so many commercials and options; there is no
silence to allow us thought.

In my first year as a financial advisor, I looked past
Social Media and the internet to tear through the networking
circuit with reckless abandon. Night-in and night-out I would
attend a new networking function. These events were typically
sponsored by a local chamber of commerce. All attendees
would show up to mix and mingle, with the main goal of
handing out and collecting as many business cards as possible.
The theme I found at most of the ones I attended was that my
new friends were either unemployed, freshly laid off, looking
for a job, or starting a brand new business. At the end of the

[22] Proceedings of The National Academy of Sciences- 2013
[23] MacLeans- "Why We Need to Clear Our Cluttered Minds", Jonathon
Gatehouse, 2014

day, we were all people that needed a lot of help! You could call this our industry's version of "speed dating". Great quantity of prospects, easy to obtain, but the quality would leave something to be desired.

These run in's would typically go like this... "Heyy Joey, how ya been brother?" with a big slap on the back.

"Oh boy I'll tell ya what Bry, been busy as hell," as he just started his third job in the past two months, "This year's killing me, not enough time in the day you know what I mean. But man we are raking it in with the business. How's life on your end?"

"You're telling me. It's the same here, totally swamped at the office, can't even see beyond the workload," said after a long day at the office with no meetings and 100 cold calls, "But better than the alternative right!"

Misery indeed loves company. Many of these events seemed like a dark pit of people at a low point who needed a partner to commiserate with. I was lucky enough to meet a few diamonds in the rough to keep my career on life support, but it didn't take me long to realize I had to start getting picky with those I surrounded myself with, or I wouldn't take off the way I imagined.

Networking's purpose is this... proximity to power is empowerment. Successful business people crawl through the weeds to get to the roses. I forced my way into circles of the proverbial movers and shakers. These guys played golf and hung out at political gatherings, charity benefits, and award galas. Befriend the "Connector", the bigwig that people gravitate towards. Compared to the speed dating outlet, this was like manning up and asking the dime to dance at homecoming.

While I may have only been 22 years old and looking more like 16 years old, a few principles were instrumental at such social occasions...

- The Book of Samurai mentioned, "Meet even those you know in a first time manner and you shall have no bad relationships. When guests are leaving, the mood of being reluctant to say farewell is essential." It may be thousands of years old, but this quote is spot on. In my beginning days, right after the crooked mentors were fired, I would take some of our best senior advisors out on client appointments. When we welcomed our clients into our office they would greet the husband and wife with a huge smile and firm handshake, or for some a bear hug and kiss. Before we ever entered a conference room, the clients would feel at ease. Your first impression may not make the deal, but it certainly can ruin it. The meetings would proceed in whichever manner they may, but as long as we opened and closed with a bang, we were golden.
- Build reciprocity. There's a saying, "A Sicilian does not do favors, but accumulates debts." Most recent grads will only have a few connections, so be prepared to give before you get.

A couple of other quick tips:

- Be prepared... Mistakes may be excused, but being unprepared is NEVER one of them. Running late, forgetting your tie, a poor presentation- all are forbidden. When I purchased the $100 ticket to attend the latest hoopla, I made it a point to familiarize myself with as many attendees before I showed up, typically through online espionage. I never wanted to walk into the big gala by myself without knowing anyone to speak to and lacking conversation topics. This included going through guest lists, committee volunteers, sponsor ads, etc. and then researching each name I found. (For further instruction, watch the scene from Wedding Crashers where Owen Wilson and Vince Vaughn pose as a maple syrup conglomerate to fit in with the elegant crowd.)

- Stay current... A reputed expert cannot afford to be baffled by a common question in front of new acquaintances. "Can you believe the way that IPO bolstered the market today?"- Rich guy. "Uhhhh what IPO?"- Alleged financial guru. I always tell our new class of agents to listen to Bloomberg radio on the way to the appointment; you can blast Taylor Swift on the way home.

- Keep in touch... Mark Granovetter said in 1974 in his book *Getting a Job*, that acquaintances are more important than friends because it is those weak ties that can introduce to us new crowds. After all, our friends occupy only the same world we do.

- Your bridges... do NOT burn them. Don't ever screw anyone on the way up, because you'll never know when you need them on the way down.

- Take charge... in 1727 a 21 year old printer from Philadelphia named Ben was looking to get his name out there and meet the right people. He formed a club called *Junto*, a forum to debate questions of morals, politics, philosophy, and more. The idea was to create a self-improvement group with a representative from each different profession in town. These men met every Friday night and quickly expanded the group. Ben wanted to make a change so he became a leader, and the rest is American history.

- Fake it until you make it… Before creating Junto, Ben Franklin arrived in America with a Dutch Dollar and one Schilling. He offered this as a tip to his boatmen, the man refused. Franklin forced them to take it anyway. "A man is sometimes more generous when he has little money than when he has plenty, perhaps through fear of being thought to have but little," he said.

That was me. I would get invited by my new friends to all these benefits and galas. "Sure, I'd be glad to attend. What's it, $200 per ticket, count me in, and oh add one more for my girlfriend too!" I would show up at these functions to benefit underprivileged high school kids, *man that's not too far of a stretch from me!* Hell I was serving as The Chairman of The Board of Directors for a local YMCA, people would see my poster hanging above the entrance and didn't know who I was, because I couldn't yet afford the gym membership!

It didn't take long before I was sitting on Committees for numerous charities, providing counsel to township economic development boards, and most importantly acting as the sole steward for millions of dollars of my clients' life savings. "Exactly how old are you?" a few bold would ask, while 100% of the rest obviously pondered. This sort of age discrimination would haunt me for a while. Sometimes I'd look away and mumble 23, hoping they'd soon forget. More often I'd lie and go with 27, not sure why but that was my go to age, and they'd shake their heads and conversation would carry on. "You should not consider a man's age, but his acts." Sophocles said this in Antigone. Validating him should be the goal of any young professional.

These are a few of the fundamentals you must take with you on your quest towards your first million... stay prepared and current, practice reciprocity, be polite and remember the manners we learned in kindergarten, find the "Connectors", givers gain (BNI), be a leader, never burn your bridges, keep in touch, and always open and close on the right note.

Life is nothing more than a series of uncontrollable coincidences. But how you react to these coincidences and the decisions then made are what shape life. Had you stayed in that night rather than hit the bar with your pals, would you have bumped into that girl when you screamed at the Giants touchdown, would you have exchanged numbers after she made fun of you, would you have introduced her friend to your brother who then married her? You get the idea. We never know who knows who and how things will turn out. Being a part of the game is what makes it all possible.

So when do you start getting active? Now! Careers can soar on relationships that were built in middle school. Millennials all too often wait until their thirties to "start life". That's more than a third of your life spent "getting ready". Keep in mind, the document that founded this great country, The Declaration of Independence, was authored by a 33 year-old Thomas Jefferson. If that's not motivation enough, look at it this way... Earth is an estimated 4.543 billion years old, American life expectancy is approximately 78 years, which means you have less than a split second of Earth's time to make an impact, get on it!

<u>Step 6: Get a Head Start</u>

*"Make mistakes of ambition not sloth,
strength to be bold not suffer..."
- Machiavelli*

Old clients say two things on a consistent basis, "I must have gotten up like ten times to go to the bathroom last night," and, "Jeez, I wish we had done this sooner." Wealth managers can't help with the bathroom thing, but we can do our best to inspire other youngsters to take advantage of our greatest asset, time. Unless you were born at a very young age, NOW is the time to start planning.

Ben Franklin's famous almanac provides tips on how to be more efficient and productive early on. His "Plan for Future Conduct", which by the way, he authored at twenty years old, promotes four steps designed for a young professional, but applicable to any age...

1. It is necessary for me to be extremely frugal for some time, till I have paid what I owe.
2. To endeavor to speak truth in every instance; to give nobody expectations that are not likely to be answered, but aim at sincerity in every word and action (the most amiable excellence in a rational being).
3. To apply myself industriously to whatever business I take in hand, and not divert my mind from my business by any foolish project of suddenly growing rich; for industry and patience are the surest means of plenty.
4. I resolve to speak ill of no man whatever.

Successful people spend most of their adult life at work, hopefully enjoying that work, but let's be real the paycheck is a major factor. Please take a few hours away from Call of Duty, and look at your monetary situation and future goals. Perfection does not exist and therefore the time to start is never going to be perfect. "Someday" is a disease that will take your dreams to the grave with you.

How do you start? - The oldest mantra in financial planning is to "Pay Yourself First!" This one phrase could cure so many of the economic difficulties that plague our country today, and the world for that matter. We can all remember the golden years of college... babes, booze, and ramen noodles. My buddies and I would run from class Friday afternoon, pumped for the excitement of the weekend. Typically we'd each have $100 or so in our pocket from whatever little part time work we'd done during the week, more than enough for dorm life. The weekend would commence, but somehow we'd all reconvene Sunday night with empty pockets.

"Dude where the hell did my 100 bucks go!?" We'd map out each step we could recollect from the weekend, like a chick who lost her first diamond earrings. "Well let's see I paid five bucks to get in the frat party Friday, I think we ordered late night Chinese for like $10, Saturday we bought a thirty pack and..." Man I can't remember, but it's all gone. And so this process would repeat, every weekend.

These dollars that mysteriously leak out of our financial world go on eternally, for households, businesses, and government. It's the lack of keeping a budget, or sticking to it more importantly. As Ben Franklin said, "Beware of expenses, a small leak will sink a great ship."

Wealthy people pay themselves first (preferably at a rate of 20% of income), and then the rest is easy. We pay Uncle Sam first don't we? The treasury doesn't ask for money at the end of the month, they pay themselves first! Mr. and Mrs. Young Professional, if you're saving $200 monthly here and investing $300 monthly over there, I don't give a rat's ass where the rest goes. This philosophy will immediately defeat Parkinson's Law- expenses rising to meet newfound income.

Once you do start investing, at a young age, the magic begins to happen. It's called compounding. If you don't believe in compounding, please go speak to any thirty year old who recklessly opened a credit card in college. They will acquaint you with compounding interest. Now how would you like to be the credit card company as opposed to that poor schlep crawling out of the quick sand?

The second most important advice for young professionals, after starting saving/investing habits early, is to stay liquid. Guys and gals a year or two out of college land their first real job, and bam they go buy the brand new Mercedes or Range Rover. Now they have a huge payment and they're starting to inherit some of their own expenses as they move out and grow up. The solution to this new, tight budget is plastic. Credit cards that can't be zeroed out at the end of the month are POISON.

To piggyback on this point, the next chronological step too often rushed is purchasing a home. We all want to be homeowners and that time will come, but make sure you are ready. Countless young couples with big eyes buy their dream house and scrounge up the largest down payment possible. Now they are immediately thrust into a temporary situation of being House Rich and Cash Poor, but it will only be *temporary* right? Hang on though, the house is empty. And wait, that shower and sink hardly work. Time to buy all this furniture *and* renovate the bathroom, but there's hardly any cash left. "Excuse me Mr. Plumber; do you accept a credit card? Jason's Furniture and Best Buy both helped us with a personal credit card you know." All of a sudden the shrinking rainy day fund is lost for decades.

A year or two down the road Mr. and Mrs. Young Professional spend in the ballpark of $30-$40,000 on their wedding, as we do up in the Northeast. That one day is so expensive, and the credit cards have already been used up so much, that the only source of funds they can find are that 401(k) they didn't know they were auto enrolled into. Now instead of paying high interest rates to the credit card company, they pay income taxes and a steep 10% early withdrawal penalty to open the lockbox intended for retirement.

There truly is good debt and bad debt. It's imperative you recognize their differences. A mortgage is a good form of debt, typically providing a low-fixed interest rate, and tax write offs. This kind of debt is favored to virtually any other (student loans, auto loans, furniture loans, CREDIT CARDS, etc.) Also remember, you will always have a "mortgage", it's called property taxes. So get used to the bill. A home is often a family's greatest asset, so please be careful in financing this investment. If you can't walk away from the closing table with your three to six months rainy day fund intact, seriously reconsider.

The solution to liquidity lies within this "Rainy Day Fund" or as I like to call it a "Sunny Day Opportunity Fund". The rule of thumb is three to six months gross income or expenses readily available. Three months is acceptable for a dual income household, in which there isn't so much pressure on one spouse to produce. If that isn't the case, and there is a breadwinner and homemaker, six months cushion can take a lot of worry off of the rainmaker. Cash is king and don't forget it.

***

Beyond these basic cash flow habits, a strict "Protection First" mentality is paramount. Clients should save/invest, stay liquid, make money, and grow rich, but unfortunately some factors are out of our control. Do you know what your biggest asset really is? Hint: it's not your cars, home, jewelry, or 401(k). For a young professional, the foundation of all financial planning is income, both now and in the future. Your ability to earn an income trumps all else. Insure the Golden Goose (you) and not just those golden eggs.

If you get sick or hurt, the most efficient way to protect your income and lifestyle, bar none, is Disability Insurance, or as I call it "Income Insurance". Customers protect what they love not what they fear. We buy Auto Insurance, not Crash Insurance. We buy Life Insurance, not Death Insurance. We buy Homeowner's Insurance, not Fire Insurance.

Imagine what pockets you would tap, God forbid the unexpected should occur... Mom and Dad? Government (Social Security)? Your "Sunny Day Fund"? Work? Individual Disability Insurance? Let's take a look...

- Mom and Dad- You've worked all your life and earned that education and unique skill set so that one day you would be independent. Plus, they'll have their own problems to deal with; soon we'll discuss how they live forever and accidentally spend down your inheritance.

- Social Security- The fact of the matter is that most claims are denied. Social Security uses what's called an "Any Occupation" definition of disability. In English, you can't be gainfully employed and must be unable to perform *any* occupation to actually qualify for this benefit. If this definition is enough to satisfy you, just remember the current shape of our Social Security system (see Step 3).
- "Sunny Day Fund"- while this is supposed to be the slush fund, most of us have some sort of earmark in the back of our head for this random checking account: vacation, kids' college, condo in Florida, and so forth. Even if you were disciplined enough to save 10% of your paycheck for ten straight years into a restricted account, in only one year of disability you would wipe out those ten years of savings!
- Work- some employees are lucky enough to be covered by a Group LTD (Long-Term Disability) Plan. This is often confused with STD (Short-Term Disability) which provides a relatively small benefit for up to a maximum of 26 weeks; or Aflac, which is strictly a supplement. Unfortunately, as the cost of doing business and providing health benefits skyrockets, these plans are becoming rarer. If you are covered, there may be many strings attached. Most group plans today are "Any Occupation" or "Modified Own Occupation" defined. This is a strict definition that prohibits any other income during disability and does not clearly define your occupation. Disability can have a lot of grey area, and the horror stories come out when you thought you

were covered, but when you need it most the insurance carrier sends you and your family a denial letter. These benefits may also be taxable and capped at a certain amount. Be careful physicians, salesman, and traders... your Group LTD will usually cover base pay only; even though most of your income may be performance-based. The majority of group plans are also not portable, meaning that if you were to leave this job for another down the road, the insurance stays and you go naked. Bear in mind, The Bureau of Labor Statistics says the average American worker stays at one job for only 4.4 years[24]!

- Individual Disutility Insurance- this is the kind I recommend for most professionals, especially entrepreneurs, physicians, and people with job mobility. A "True Own Occupation" definition is preferable, as this attempts to make disability claims as black and white as possible. Such a definition states that if you cannot perform the material and substantial duties of your own occupation, even if you're gainfully employed elsewhere, you will be deemed disabled. Another feature that is important is that because it's being funded with post-tax dollars, any indemnity would be received 100% tax free. It is also critical to look for a policy that is Non-Cancellable/ Guaranteed Renewable. This means the policy is 100% portable, no matter how you change your occupation, employer, or geographical location, this one stays with you. Also, your rates are guaranteed to never change, regardless of your health, age, or how the insurance company is faring in the

---

[24] Bureau of Labor Statistics- 2012

economy. You are locked in. Lastly, the rider young professionals should obtain is what's called a Future Insurability Option (FIO). This allows the insured to continue purchasing additional coverage throughout their career without any underwriting or evidence of insurability, at the same rating they got when they were young and healthy.

Income protection could deserve its own chapter. Let me tell you why I decided to make a True Own Occupation Disability Policy a part of my financial plan. In my first couple of years in the business I was proud to show friends my plan and educate them how to do the same. One of our partners, this fossil, would always get on my case that I was missing the most important piece. He went on to tell me that financial planning is not an exact science; rather we're trying to eliminate mistakes and mitigate risks for our clients...

"To purchase Individual Disability Insurance and go your whole career paying that premium to only one day retire in good health, without career interruption, in the scheme of things that fraction of your income that you paid each year was a small mistake. But to forego Disability Insurance, and one day down the road when you have a family, house, and business depending on your income... God forbid you did get sick or hurt and couldn't come to work, then it's a COLOSSAL mistake. Finance is all about trading big mistakes for little mistakes. Now don't be cheap!" he said.

That made sense from an economic stand point. But I still dragged my feet as a young, healthy marathoner and Ironman. Shortly thereafter I was hosting one of my Financial Education workshops for the medical residents at Raritan Bay

Medical Center. My mentor tagged along, at the end of my spiel he shared a story I never forgot. From Howard:

"I had a client of mine who was the managing partner at a huge law firm in the city (NYC). He would make anywhere from $600,000-$800,000 depending on the year. He was thriving and lived a lifestyle to go along with it, big house, three kids in private schools, and so on. I advised him for several years, managing assets and helping with his estate plans. Every year during an annual review I would bust his chops for not having Disability Insurance, *You're Nuts*, I yelled at him, *you're running around naked with a huge firm and loving family depending on you.* Every year he would politely decline, *Howard I'm good man. I'm healthy as a horse, I run three miles a day before I come to the office, and I got nothing to fret over. Hell even if I lost my legs in an accident, I'd come to work in a wheel chair because I love practicing law.*

After countless attempts, the client finally obliged, partly to shut me up. We covered $800,000 of income with True Own Occupation Individual Disability Insurance, mostly through The Guardian and some with Lloyds of London.

Exactly two years to the day after I placed that policy, I received a call from his assistant. *Howard I hate to bother you but I have a quick question.* I said of course, kind of a random call. *Did you ever place a Disability Insurance policy with my boss?* I was taken aback but replied yes and asked if everything is ok. *No I need to speak with you about it.* I was shocked of all my clients, he was invincible. I asked "What's wrong?" *Well three months ago my boss's son was killed in a car accident, and he hasn't come back to work since.*

I was shocked, like the wind got knocked right outta me. We immediately filed a claim for mental/nervous disorder and that claim paid. It's one of the saddest stories I've experienced in my career, but imagine where his family would have been without that policy."

For me that did it. I finally came to grips that there are thousands of reasons why someday I might not be able to come to work and do what I do. Consumers must accept that insurance, regardless of the type, is the only financial product you are not assured of getting tomorrow. It doesn't matter... Until it matters... Then it's all that matters.

***

So far we've mentioned two of the building blocks to your foundation, Cash and Insurance. The final and third happens to be Estate Planning. This is essentially the playbook of your entire estate, all that you are, materially and immaterially. The intricacies of Estate Planning are outside the scope of this book, but put it this way... If you're married, or if you have children, and you're running around without a properly drafted Will, to me that says you don't care what happens when your time's up. Don't be selfish.

The biggest objection to thinking ahead with Estate Planning is the sour fact that we don't want to admit the end. There are countless attorneys who don't even have a Will. You can do it for yourself for free! "We're young, we've got time. My wife doesn't want to discuss it." The excuses are never-ending. I hate to burst your bubble, but there are only two guarantees in this life, and Death is one of them.

Is there a facet of Financial Planning that's even less addressed, and usually harder to attend to than death? Yes! What if Barbie and Ken wake up one day and the mojo has disappeared. The sad circumstance is that approximately 50% of marriages today end in divorce.

Every sound plan has its contingencies. A wedding is typically the most expensive day of your life; if that's false you've probably experienced a divorce. When a divorce happens, there is only one winner, and that's the attorney. The judge will wipe away your tears with your own checkbook.

Anyone with substantial assets entering a marriage should strongly consider Prenuptial Arrangements. This is perhaps the most depressing thought leading up to the happiest moment, but it's reality. I hate to see a successful client enter into their second or third marriage, only to say, "No way am I getting prenups, this is the one, I'm so happy I've finally found love." A short year or two later, half of his life's work vanishes.

There are a few things to consider when you're getting started in the real world... Start saving now, not later. No need to keep up with the Jones', take your time on all those purchases. Stay away from the credit cards! Lock up your insurability. Draft a Will. And think long and hard before you buy those rings, roughly 75% of divorces in America happen before turning thirty[25]!

The word "Balance" is spoken countless times in any financial dialogue. Clients should strive to strike a balance between living for today and saving for tomorrow. There are two surefire ways to failure in financial planning, worry about

---

[25] Office of National Statistics- 2012

tomorrow and neglect today, or worry about today and neglect tomorrow. As Euripides said in Rhesus, "Slight not what is near through aiming at what is far."

We all remember our grandparents; they were the last people we got to know intimately who already experienced each phase of life. Their lives generally consisted of go to work, put in your time, don't spend what you don't have, and then you'll be taken care of. Those amenities don't exist anymore.

Lastly, ask yourself if life has gone just as you planned. Take a brief look back at our still new millennium... the indomitable "Dot Com Bubble" burst, Apple created the iPod, terrorists devastated our country with airplanes, the Euro entered circulation, Myspace started social media, USA entered two wars, Facebook was launched, YouTube, NetFlix replaced TV, Hurricane Katrina created a third world in the new world, Saddam Hussein was executed, Apple debuted iPhone, Amazon produced an E-book, worldwide recession, the first black president, Osama Bin Laden killed, Joe Paterno fired, and Hurricane Sandy rewrote the meaning of Flood Insurance.

I don't know anyone who was not completely shocked by the events above. So embrace the fact that we are going to be utterly blindsided again in the future, again, and again.

Step 7: Draft The Right Players

"Whenever you purpose to consult with anyone about your affairs, first observe how he has managed his own; for he who has shown poor judgment in conducting his own business will never give wise counsel about business of others."
- Socrates (Letter to Demonicus)

There are three kinds of prospective clients. One- I don't want anyone knowing my affairs, I'll handle this all myself. Two- I got an A+ in my Principles of General Accounting 101, believe me I've forgotten more than you know. Three- Please help me. *Sadly, there's an even bigger contingent of "I could care less" people, but they're not reading this book and our taxes will bail them out anyway.*

The smartest and most successful folks are the ones who know what they don't know. For those of you who are open minded and want to stay up-to-date on your financial situation, this chapter may be a guide to your guide. Financial advisors are no longer purely for rich people. Believe me, there's enough of us to go around. So who do you pick? That's a great question.

It is funny how if you attend any of those networking events; you'll find millions of advisors. All of us are going by the exact same name and pretty much using the same tagline. If there are so many of us, why the epidemic of financial education? I think it's because "Financial Advisor" is one of the easiest titles to hang on your shingle, similar to being a realtor. As the US Bureau of Labor Statistics pointed out earlier, it's a career with "low barriers to entry".

For instance, I've encountered numerous clients ready and willing to implement certain investment products, who in the past were unable to do so because their former advisors lacked the necessary securities licenses. Such clients were then restricted to the product competency of that advisor. Talk about trying to fit a round peg into a square hole.

My agency for example, has ten Financial Advisors to my knowledge. However throughout the years we have had 100's of "Financial Advisors" pass through. According to FINRA, in 2005 there were a baffling 48 different designations a financial adviser could obtain. Throw in some new regulations and a financial meltdown, and that number soared to 95 professional designations in 2010[26]!

Ever hear of a CFA? How about a CRFA? They sound the same don't they? The former, Chartered Financial Analyst, requires 900 hours of study in various areas of accounting/finances and completion of three six-hour exams (with just a 45% pass rate). The latter, Certified Retirement Financial Adviser, is a paltry 100 question multiple choice exam.

How about a RSA, LUTCF, ChFC, CLU, ABC123 perhaps? Our industry has become flooded with more licenses and designations than professionals can track, let alone the average customer. In conversations of taxes, there is usually one single resource, your trusted CPA (Certified Public Accountant). So why, when it comes time for the client to actually move their money and life savings, is there a constellation of alphabet soup?

---

[26] Financial Industry Regulatory Authority- 2010

Wait, we're not done yet. There exists another assembly of advisors who attempt to skirt compliance by creating their *own* designations. You may have received a call recently to have your retirement portfolio reviewed by a "Financial Architect", "Monetary Engineer", or "Economic Designer". You might be laughing right now, and you should be. These labels are more often used by insurance salesmen as they fly under the radar of the securities industry. The Wall Street Journal has identified over another 115 designations that FINRA does not track[27]. As you may be realizing, the less education and licensing you have, the more you are able to speak freely and tout nonexistent knowledge.

Did you know there are even part-time *Financial Advisors*!? These agents are made famous by various multi-level marketing programs. The first question to them is often, "Financial Advisor- that's great, are you Full-Time or Part-Time?" The vast majority regrettably are part-time. The process often goes like this... Call your friends and family, inquire to their life insurance situation, sell them Term Life Insurance, ask for referrals, and then immediately offer the new client a position to be a *Financial Advisor* with your company. The spread of financial education is important, but misinformation can be as harmful as no information. The bulk of these *experts* I've come across are stay at home mom's, personal trainers looking for a side gig, or people involved in a whole array of pyramid schemes, bouncing from a Tupper Ware meeting to a financial planning consultation.

---

[27] "Is Your Advisor Pumping Up His Credentials", Wall Street Journal- 2010

I am extremely proud to say that the industry is making some attempts to untangle the mayhem. The media has played a large role in popularizing the CFP® (Certified Financial Planner™). Many equate the CFP® to the CPA. In order to use these letters after your name, one must have at least three years of experience in the field, a sponsor/mentor, a clean record, and then pass six college style courses with final exams, present to an expert panel for approval, and then sit for the daunting ten hour board exam with a less than 60% pass rate. Only then can a financial planner truly be certified. Please visit www.cfp.net for additional information. On the investment side, clients should become familiar with FINRA's website "Broker Check". This will tell you the good, the bad, the ugly on your financial advisor.

The most common horror stories involve Grandma and Grandpa. This is an area of financial planning that can spell calamity, frequently an age bracket with the most money, but mental faculties beginning to fade. Investment News wrote an article in 2013 (Seniors Baffled by Raft of Specialty Designations) that went on to address over fifty designations catered *specifically* to seniors[28]! At a stage of life where simplicity and transparency are vital, can we confuse these poor old-timers anymore?

***

If you've followed the previous steps and now feel ready for some professional direction, here are some pointers in your search for a financial steward...

---

[28] "Seniors Baffled by Raft of Specialty Designations", U.S. News- 2013

You are *hiring* a Financial Planner. Akin to any employer, interview your help. I have a client who happens to be an old Jewish businessman, and well-to-do. He felt that his previous advisor was approaching retirement and starting to neglect his sizeable account. After a few years of pursuing this prospect, he phoned me and said it's time for a change.

I entered our first meeting, ready to give my brief guff (or Unique Value Proposition as we call it) and dive into Fact Finding. After thirty seconds of small talk, the prospect cut me off and said, "Ok Bryan, thanks for coming out today. But before we get into any sort of planning or questionnaire, I have my own process as a client and it begins with an interview." He proceeded to pull out a typed up letter with fifteen questions on it. They ranged from *Who do you represent and potential conflicts of interests, How are you paid, Why did you become a financial planner, what profession are most of your clients in, etc.* What a turn of the table? Maybe that's why his accounts have so many zeros.

Another trait in higher net worth clients was getting to know who I was, far beyond work. One of my clients is in his late sixties with a big belly and even bigger ego. He was the retired type who you knew had our meeting highlighted on his calendar weeks in advance. Even though he didn't work and was always coming to my office from home, he still made it a point to show up in his sharpest suit and tie. Throughout our meetings he would play devil's advocate to all of my recommendations, while his sweet wife sat there in silence. Somewhere between my recommendations and getting the check, we seemed to have hit a standstill.

Tim called me one day, "Bryan, Samantha and I would love to go out to dinner with you and your wife." Now I didn't have a wife yet, you people are three times my age dude. But I did arrange a nice dinner with my girlfriend at a local Italian joint. After a few bottles of wine and him ordering the whole menu, I got a call the following morning, "Thanks a lot for dinner that was a blast! We'll be by tomorrow with your check."

Small business clients agree that one of the scariest phases of their life is walking away from their work, the *Exit Strategy*. The rest of the W-2 world goes through the same process, they call it *Retirement*. It's the first time when we stop the daily routine, sit back, look at our life's earnings, and say "Ok, now what the heck do we do with this?" We will differentiate later the *Accumulation Phase* vs. the *Distribution Phase*, but when we transition from depending on ourselves, to depending on our money, it can be a bit frightening.

Most financial planning prospects initially tell me, "Thanks Bry, but I got a guy." Everyone's "got a guy". So I'm provoked to ask them, "That's outstanding you have some professional help, but what's your *guy's* exit strategy." The befuddled look hits them, "I have no idea, his business isn't my business." Wrong!

When you hang it up and decide to retire to the lodge in Maine, your trusted advisor is probably doing the same thing down on the links in Florida. The Distribution Phase is a whole other stage of life, sometimes outlasting our working years. Help then is as vital as it is now.

I used to be reluctant to share with a client how old I was. Until a CPA who refers me some business told my mentor,

I only want to work with Bryan because when I walk away he's going to be hitting his stride.

Other client tips:

- Keep an open mind. Conventional wisdom, is as the name implies, that which is comfortable. 90% of the population enjoys the comfort peddled by major media, while the other 10% enjoy the money raised unconventionally. We all have our own viewer bias, that's why we listen to particular news channels and remember the stories that support our already existing ideals. That's fine, but check it at the door when you're ready to learn. Don't forget that average is not always safe, and unorthodox is not always risky.

- "Speak English!"- That's another one I hear a lot. Most would agree that complex ideas must be made simple, or they'll just remain ideas and never be put into action. There's no point in having the best advisor, if you can't understand him or her. First time clients should ask questions, and if they're not answered concisely and in plain English, don't worry you're not stupid rather that's probably a red flag. There are plenty of professionals who use fast talk and industry jargon as a cover for incompetence.

- Or "Don't Speak English!"- We have a Korean office, a Greek corner, and a Hasidic Jew branch. People are starving for comfort, typically found by their brethren. If the guidance is valuable and your advisor meets the basic criterion, there's nothing wrong with choosing a CFP® whom you could call a buddy.

- "What's your FICO Score?"- I've worked out all my life, from peewees to college sports to an international Ironman. Every gym has a female trainer that looks like she belongs on the cover of a magazine, or the male trainer that could beat up Hercules, they always have clients. There are also the trainers with beer bellies and a slouched gait, they rarely have clients. If your advisor is not practicing what they preach, it is a big problem. I've worked alongside advisors in my office that have spiffy suits and talk a big game, but were actually on unemployment during a freeze in their contract! Don't be shy to ask what your advisor's plan looks like, and what their personal ups and downs in the economy have been. Make the transparency a two way street.
- Finally, seek an advisor who strives for success with significance, not only money. That's why I loved my one client's interview; it forced me to reveal my passions. Find an advisor who's excited. Genuine excitement and passion go hand in hand. Sitting down with the wet rag may not only be boring, but an advisor who's not emotionally invested probably isn't giving you the latest and best service either.

A trustworthy advisor's introduction should start with... A) Who Am I? B) Who Do I Work For? C) How Do I Get Paid? D) How Do We Get Started? This is a designed sequential order, if there is disagreement at a certain step; the following are a moot point.

In summary, 1) Interview your "guy". 2) It's ok to ask who they are beyond a spread sheet. 3) If they are young qualify their experience, but if they are old inquire about their practice transition. 4) Keep an open mind. 5) Demand he or she speak English (or whatever makes sense to you). 6) Ask to see their financial plan. 7) Find passion in your advisor. Ask **"Who are you and why are you?"**

***

By now you've realized that you want to work with a proficient CFP® who meets the above qualifications, but *where* do you find them? The largest clients stem from referrals, or word of mouth.

The most common Centers of Influence whom advisors collaborate with, and would recommend you listen to when seeking the right CFP®, fall into a few categories... your Property and Casualty Agent (particularly for business owners), your CPA, your Estate Attorney/Trust Officer, or your Banker.

However, you should be aware that your "most trusted advisor", the Certified Public Accountant, may also be getting paid for his introduction.

Adopted in 1998, N.J.A.C. 13:29-3.8 and 3.12 allowed CPAs to clean up. This is arguably the most impactful law regarding cross marketing since the passage of Graham-Leach-Bliley, which combined traditional banking and investment banking. If I receive a referral from say an attorney, the best I can do is thank them or maybe offer a nice lunch under $100. But, did you know that your accountant is allowed to hold Insurance and Securities Licenses. Therefore, I'm happy to pay licensed CPA's who refer me their clients up to 50% of the commissions I make.

You will be hard pressed to find an accounting firm, from the Big Four down to your local Mom and Pop that has not looked to exploit this new revenue stream. Critics continue to debate its efficacy, considering multiple cooks in the kitchen possibly contaminating a client centric relationship. There should be more clarity or disclosure in the CPA's commission opportunities when he/she encourages his client to suddenly sit with this Insurance or Stock Broker.

***

Now, to key you in on some of the things going on behind the scenes... Akin to most prominent businesses, we are not exempt from following the Paretto Principle. 80% of our business does come from 20% of our clients. It's foolish not to focus on this statistic, so advisors categorize their clients into their A's, B's, and C's.

Regarding the Paretto Principle, effective advisors must be cutthroat with their time. This is not to disservice the client, but actually to provide help equally to all clients and referrals. Not to mention that our industry has become so encumbered with regulation and paperwork that the addition of each new client creates at least two to four hours of initial onboarding, this is beyond the entire planning process and future service. Therefore, I can accept yes's and no's, but not maybe's. A client should never feel rushed into a decision, but commission based advisors can't sit on the China Egg all day waiting for it to hatch. Sometimes inaction can be more harmful than action. Such speed of transaction makes Emergency Room physicians ideal clients, and conversely engineering professionals repeatedly overlooked.

No matter what classification of client you may be, you need to tell us what's going on! I can remember my parents grumbling how frustrating it was to bring me and my brother to the doctor when we were toddlers, because the physician could run his tests, but other than a burp or fart there wasn't much communication. Now as grownups, we go into the doctor's office and complete a questionnaire before we even meet. If a doctor doesn't do a thorough workup and carelessly prescribes some medicine, he is of course subject to malpractice. Financial people have the same liability (Errors and Omissions) and it all starts with a fact finder. When it comes to money, people are uncomfortable getting undressed. We need to speak English to you, please don't hide the facts from us.

A primary goal of experienced advisors is not only uncovering needs and establishing rapport, but managing expectations from the outset. Clients frequently enter a financial firm with visions of grandeur and sexy stock tips. The worst case scenario is when the advisor responds and promises the world. The best salesmen are those who can under promise, over deliver, and keep the client content all the way. So don't buy hook line and sinker into all that, "You name it, you got it. I'll have you swimming in gold coins" hogwash.

Advisors have a unique lifestyle outside the conference room too. The gentleman who recruited me out of college told me in our first interview that for the "First five years you're going to be way overworked and way underpaid. Then for the next 35 years you're going to be way underworked, and way overpaid." This stressful dynamic may not have anything to do with it, but my associates have a tough time keeping a marriage together. All the senior advisors in my office and most I know at the other locations are on their second marriage or have gone through at least a couple of divorces. This might not affect any client-advisor decision making, but it is an odd similarity in older colleagues.

It is a taxing business on our side, as it usually is for most entrepreneurs. It is tough putting our mind to rest when we're concerned with not just our finances but those of many others. How we all react to the failures and successes of the career is distinctive to each of us.

In summary, it's ok to seek help. Think about your money in the same fashion you would any other aspect of your life you deem important. How do you choose a doctor? How do you pick what day care to send your baby to? How do you hire, fire, and promote within your own organization. Don't make it more complicated than it needs to be. Finally, don't skimp on researching your future fiduciary, remember the saying "Quis custodiet ipsos custodies?"- from *Juvenal*. Latin for "Who will guard the guards".

<u>Step 8: Invest in What You Know</u>

"Whenever you find yourself on the side of the majority,
it is time to pause and reflect."
- Mark Twain

It was the summer of 2005 and we had recently graduated high school. A few buddies and I decided to take a day off from being beach bums and spice things up with a trip to Six Flags.

After paying $15 to park, I navigated my old, champagne colored Ford Taurus through rows of charter buses and endless bags of trash.   We proceeded to enter the park and target the best roller coasters, half of which were closed for repairs. The high diving show was cancelled, the overpriced burgers tasted like hockey pucks, and most ride attendants didn't speak English. "Dude this place turned into a mess", my one buddy said. We made a quick exit and crossed Six Flags off the things to do list.

Two years later, I was readying for my junior year at TCNJ. I worked a long summer, lifeguarding during the day and slicing meats and cheeses at the local Wegman's deli by night. I built up a nice little cushion in the bank and decided it was time for my money to go to work as well. September 20, 2007 I proudly deposited $500 into a Scottrade account, "Here come the big bucks", I thought.

I excitedly combed through financial magazines and ratings agencies, trying to locate the stock worthy of my money. I used a screener for stocks trading under $10 per share with a four or five star Morningstar rating. I scoured through them looking for a familiar name, BAM, there it was, ticker symbol SIX- Six Flags Class B trading at $3.33. Five-Star, AAA, Strong Buy, layup that fit exactly what I was looking for. The financials told me this was an undervalued steal.

I listened to the market experts, but in the back of my head was my buddy's voice, "Dude this place turned into a mess." All I could envision was garbage, broken rides, long lines, disgusting food, and people screaming and cursing at each other. *But man, these were the masterminds!* Time to buy my first stock.

Fast forward a couple more years to June 13, 2009 and what did all the local headlines read:

"Six Flags Files for Bankruptcy"

Awesome first investment Bry. As a result of their Chapter 11 Bankruptcy proceedings, all Class B shares were eliminated. Bye bye hard working money. I failed the first and most important tenant of investing, INVEST IN WHAT YOU KNOW! Those who base decisions on principle, not public opinion, are often vindicated in due time.

***

In a recent survey by Gallup, pollers asked respondents which investments were the best. Real estate was the top pick at 31%, followed by stocks/mutual funds at 25%, gold at 19%, savings accounts and CD's followed at 15%, and 6% chose bonds[29]. But check out this statistic... if you invested $100 in

---

[29] "American Again Say Real Estate is Best Long-Term Investment", Gallup.com- 2015

gold in 1926, it would be worth about $5,455 today[30]. $100 into the average home that year, you're looking at a value of $2,839 in 2014[31]. Lastly, $100 into the stock market (even with The Great Depression and Great Recession), your money is worth $11,128[32]!

So why does the average investor suck at stocks? Ask your parents what they paid for their home twenty years ago and they can probably recount it to the penny. Then ask them what the DOW traded at that year, probably not a clue. I bet they know how their stocks ended up yesterday though. Therein lies the dilemma, market information is instantaneous and published relentlessly. Home values are evaluated with the timeframe of decades. However, the public is inundated with meaningless short-term stock gains and losses that throw emotions on a whipsaw, resulting in irrational decisions. It's not a fair comparison of investment vehicles, rather Real Estate makes us smart and Stocks make us stupid.

When doing your homework on past performance, which is not always an indicator of future performance, take into account the entire context. Regarding the study above, I hear regularly from my clients that their parents purchased their home in 1971 for $28,000 and now it's worth ten times that! Guess what a gallon of gas in 1971 averaged- 36 cents and today- roughly ten times that[33]! What sounds like a great investment may be clouded by the unassuming effects of inflation and timing.

---

[30] www.wallstreetjournal.com – 01/19/2016
[31] "US Existing Home Sales Median Prices", www.ycharts.com - 2014
[32] Measuringworth.com, DJIA 01/01/1926-01/01/2016
[33] 2014 Average

My $500 in Six Flags stock was a gamble. When clients come into my office, we do not gamble. Some customers may have "play accounts" for day trading or a new stock tip, but true investing involves the Three Legs of The Stool...

The first leg is most recognizable to the average investor- Asset Allocation. How does this particular investment compliment the overall portfolio? Look at risk tolerances, diversification, what sectors of the market are covered, etc. An old trick advisors use is "The Rule of 100". Take 100 and subtract your age, that's the percentage of your portfolio that should be invested in the markets (i.e. a thirty year old investor should have 70% equities and 30% fixed income). However, analysts are now calling it "The Rule of 115", promoting holding equities longer as people are living longer.

The second leg is commonly overlooked but always felt- Taxes. People save and invest in various vehicles, hoping to hit the right Rate of Return. Rates of return can be meaningless if Uncle Sam has his way. There are ultimately three ways investments can grow- Taxable, Tax-Deferred, or Tax-Free. Each type of account can hold the same underlying investments, but if it's Non-Qualified, Traditional IRA, or Roth IRA, the account holder can realize totally different "Real Returns". Amidst conversation with even seasoned professionals, I casually reference the upcoming tax liability on their 401(k) or Pension and receive a look of shock and anger, "What the hell are you talking about Bry!? This is my money I earned it; I already paid taxes every year while I was working!" *I understand Mr. Client, but now it's time to pay the piper; and not just on what you put in, but all those gains too.*

The third leg is key, but probably the one most ignored-Liquidity. Liquidity is your ability to gain access to your money. Vehicles have varying levels of liquidity, ranging from cash under the mattress, to cash in the checking account that we have to walk to the bank to get, to cash in the E-Trade Account we have to call and wire to receive, to cash in the equity of our home that we have to refinance in good financial standing with the appropriate interest climate to obtain, to cash in the 401(k) we have to wait until 59 ½ to touch without taking a bath. Ben Franklin once said, "If you ever want to know the value of money, go out and try to borrow some." Again, rates of return go out the window if you cannot finance the various stages of your daily life in an efficient manner.

Thus which investments are the right ones? Einstein once stated, "Reality is merely an illusion, albeit a very persistent one." Reality is crafted by the talking heads; these blabber mouths shape most investors' decisions. There are only two kinds of talking heads- The lemur with no balls, and the guy at the racetrack.

The lemur with no balls easily goes with the overall consensus. Each week his editorial comes out, he casually gives you his current assessment on the economy. There has to be some kind of new twist on it or else who would watch? Lo and behold this commentator is parroting what all the others say. He hops on the bandwagon, never jeopardizing his job because the outcast can be fired, but not the herd.

On the other hand you have the guy at the racetrack. Ever notice your one buddy at the water cooler that can't wait to tell you his story at the track Sunday, he called the 50-1 Longshot in the Exacta and nailed it! What a friggin genius!

Please disregard the absurd gambling debt he's meanwhile racked up. But this guy must be a friggin genius to have landed that Exacta!

The guy at the racetrack is the financial guru looking for a big break. Each week in his modest column he makes a bold prediction no one else would think of. Life goes on and his column maintains an audience of ten viewers. Then all of a sudden, WAMMY, the markets go soaring and flying and exploding from the most unthinkable source, and he called it! The oracle who saw it coming, crown this man immediately. He was the middle schooler launching thirty foot 3-Pointers in tryouts, knowing no one would care if he missed them, it was the impossible shot, but if it landed all eyes would be on him. These talk show hosts are making career decisions like anyone else... the lemur may be content in his job and not wanting to stir the pot, while the guy at the racetrack is still starving for his fifteen minutes of fame.

The accountability people assume for the media's financial authorities is nonexistent. When the meteorologist misses the blizzard of the century, we might face the unfortunate walk home without our snow gloves. When Cramer blows the stock tip of the week, it could cost millions of dollars in fans' portfolios. How do they discipline these experts/entertainers? Depends on their viewer ratings.

At the end of the day the media is in the business of attracting an audience. Standing the test of time, sex sells. Critics must continue to shout and tout the new and exciting. At the same time, the media is kept in business by advertisers. Read the pages of Money Magazine, notice the commercials on Squawk Box; don't think organizations are ready to neglect those who keep the lights on. I've been told a thousand times that my articles won't show up in the papers until I purchase at least a yearlong advertising campaign.

Joe Wuebben, Senior Editor of Muscle and Fitness, mentioned in a recent editorial how similar fitness and financial planning are, discussing how the best advice is always boring, and almost common sense. Be a consistent saver vs. workout four times a week, don't max out the credit cards vs. go easy on the sweets, and address every body part vs. plan comprehensively. However, the magazine cover that grabs readers' attention is *Get Shredded This Month* or *Double Your Money in the New Year*! Please resist the temptation, success lacks shortcuts.

The other mistake I made outside of not following my gut with Six Flags, was following the crowd. Warren Buffet, an envied contrarian, has made a career on finding treasure in other's trash, and trashing what other's call treasure. Good investing takes a lot of knowledge and patience, but also guts. It's never easy to pour your hard earned dollars into what the masses have coined as worthless. But savvy investors spot the diamond in the rough, they call it a discount.

Look no further than the famous cover story from Businessweek in 1979, "The Death of Equities". At the same time, Buffett strongly disagreed and happily stated that uncertainty is always the friend of the buyer. He went on with other nonbelievers to make a killing in the soaring markets of the next two decades. That famous story was published by one of the oldest and most reputable business publications standing. Forecasts can tell you a lot regarding the forecaster, but ultimately they are nothing more than opinions. And you know what they say about opinions.

Warren Buffet has routinely achieved the best of both worlds, enterprise and price. Speaking on Berkshire Hathaway, he invokes the need to secure profits on the buy not the sell, so that even a mediocre sale can still yield results. That's why I'm a fan of buying a company I like when it's at or near the 52 week low.

Lastly, when you have a stock or fund in mind, do not ignore the Gambler's Fallacy. Have you ever played the casino game of roulette? It's the one with numbers, Red and Black, and usually surrounded by hot chicks and young guys. There is the dude who puts $20 on red and says it's due to hit; they spin the little ball around andddd... BLACK! "Ah darn, what are the chances that will hit again, red's way overdue." Another $20 goes down on red, spin the ball anddd... BLACK! And so this cold streak will go on until the poor bastard has tapped out his pile. This, my friends, is "The Gambler's Fallacy". As inconceivable as it seems, black may hit fifty straight times, and the next time the fella in the tuxedo spins his little ball, it has just as good a shot of coming up again.

The Gambler's Fallacy is as prevalent in the markets as it is in Las Vegas. Investors follow their hot stocks day by day, often falling into the ruse of "It's got to turn around now, it's due!" Or perhaps listening to their favorite newscaster who's missed the past five stock tips, but has to be right soon! No professional or company is ever *due*. No matter how many times you flip a coin there is always going to be a 50% chance it hits tails. The laws of numbers apply to economics, and the risk/reward spectrum does not mind your emotions.

The markets are extremely sensitive and only relative. You can't go buy a new house or the Mom n Pop down the street tomorrow because the DOW dropped today. But Disney might be at a discount because the Fed released some news that made you shake in your boots. The markets are a fickle animal unlike any other.

Investing is one of the cornerstones of Financial Planning, but never confuse it *for* Financial Planning. Few have made their fortunes in the markets alone; it can help your cause, but don't think it's a get rich quick scheme. Hard work and economical thinking still the pave the way.

Step 9: The Psychology of Finance

"So inscrutable the arrangement of causes and consequences in this world that a 2-Penny duty on tea, unjustly imposed in a sequestered part of it, changes the conditions of all its inhabitants."- Thomas Jefferson

Are you still asking yourself, "What's it matter? Money is boring." Perhaps you are fed up with all the doom and gloom on the television, left feeling hopeless as a tiny piece of a gargantuan machine. A look back in time may unveil why from a micro and macro standpoint it does matter.

On November 11, 1918 the Armistice was signed which brought an end to The Great War (World War I); Germany had surrendered to The Allies. Several attempts at German revolution proceeded, the left attempting to model communist Russia, and the right wing nationalists furious at their government for giving up. One of these coups was led by a small group called the German Worker's Party. They soon thereafter rebranded themselves the National Socialist German Workers Party, a sort of oxymoron to attract both nationalists clinging to the right and the working class socialists of the left.

The tipping point came in 1922 and 1923 when Germany was plagued by hyperinflation. The cost of goods immediately skyrocketed as their currency became near worthless. Stories of people pushing wheelbarrows full of cash down the street to buy a loaf of bread were penned in history books. Employees' pensions disappeared overnight and middle class workers' life savings became useless, pandemonium ensued. The people clamored for any way out, with only the government to blame.

The young leader of the National Socialist German Workers Party, or NAZI's as they soon were tagged, saw this unrest as the perfect time to garner support. In November of 1923 Adolph Hitler led his party into Munich for the infamous Beer Hall Putsch.

A decade later across the Atlantic, the Great Depression rocked America. Germany was directly impacted with another economic disaster as unemployment soared yet again. The Germans finally had enough and Hitler would use this moment as a springboard to seize control with his radical ideals.

Historians will forever debate how one of the darkest dictators in history could commit such atrocities. Many point to his pure violence, others credit his incredible charisma and ability to rally the people, but it is without a doubt that economic turmoil provided his stage.

The same cycles of economies have opened the path for many other leaders, some evil and some heroic, all the way up to modern times. A more relevant example of macroeconomics was the 2008 election. Few people had any idea who Senator Barack Obama from Chicago was, let alone what he stood for. With less than a term in the Senate, he was a political rookie; and much of his personal history was hidden. But with charm and enthusiasm, he connected to the people. United with perfect timing, the Great Recession seemed to be worsening everyday leading up to the election, Americans were panicking. We didn't really know who this guy was, but he marketed himself as everything that was NOT going on in the current economy, the antithesis of George Bush. Less than a decade later, America considered electing a bonafide socialist in Bernie Sanders and a reality TV star in Donald Trump. Economic worry summons the illogical theory.

***

Proper examination of what caused these pivotal times, requires investigating where the money lies. For as long as man has been using paper, society has relied on banking institutions to be custodians of our earnings and providers of our lending. All financial institutions, such as banks, depend solely on the confidence of their customers. Once that confidence is lost, the institution must soon follow.

Imagine your back on the playground and your buddy Joey is collecting $1 from every third grader to fund the big class trip at the end of the year, Runaway Rapids! He socks away all the money in a jar under his desk. A couple of weeks later Susie from the fourth grade spots the jar and respectfully asks to borrow $5 to buy a new doll that she likes; Joey gladly lends her the money. The following week Timmy from the fifth grade follows suit and asks for $10 so he can buy the basketball he's been wanting; Joey gladly lends him the money. This continues throughout the school year, with the older kids taking and giving from the money jar. The idea becomes a hit, Christmas comes early for all of the upperclassmen. But the seasons turn and on the last day of school all of the third graders come running to Joey's desk, excited to take the jar and fund their class trip to the water park! Joey upends the jar and nine singles and a few quarters fall out. The children stare on in awe. Having lost the faith and friendship of so many classmates, Joey runs out of the classroom in tears. Class trip cancelled.

In the example above, we are the classmates, and Joey is the bank. These wardens of finance exercise what's called Fractional Reserve Banking, a banking system in which only a fraction of bank deposits are available for withdrawal[34]. This is done to expand the economy by freeing up capital that can be loaned out to other parties. Most developed countries operate under this type of system. The banks term it the *money multiplier*, others call it leverage. Realists call it depositing and withdrawing money that does not actually exist.

American banks follow a reserve requirement of 0% up to $15.2 million, 3% up to $110.2 million, and 10% over $110.2million[35]. Simply put, if I deposit $100 to my bank, they must keep $10 in cash. Where's the rest go? To your mortgage, auto loan, business loan, MasterCard, Home Depot card, etc. The banks get multiple uses of the same dollar, and at a much higher interest rate than we achieve. Sounds unfair right?

The greatest fear to any bank is the catastrophic term, "Bank Run". This is caused by too many depositors coming back to the bank and asking for their money at the same time. Lo and behold the money is not there, it does not exist. Financial experts agree that what began as a stock market crash evolved into The Great Depression, directly because of systemic bank runs... The kids wanted their money, and Joey didn't have it.

The banking industry has changed as much as any other industry throughout the ages. The Federal Depository Insurance Corporation has been put into place to insure customers' deposits up to $250,000. The Central Bank exists to back the bank down the street; God forbid there was a bank

---

[34] "Fractional Reserve Banking", Investopedia
[35] "Reserve Requirements" 01/21/2016, Federal Reserve

run. But for as many safe measures that have been enacted, there's been as many steps taken to embrace risk.

One of the most notable movements is the Graham-Leach-Bliley Act of 1999. This act of congress repealed the Glass-Steagall Act, a part of the US Banking Act of 1933. Glass-Steagall was put into place after The Great Depression in an effort to restrict activities between commercial banks and securities firms. It was meant to make finance black and white; securities firms- invest and bear risk, banks- harbor safe money.

Graham-Leach-Bliley was what many new age banks considered a Godsend. Now not only could banks lend out loads of our own money at high interest rates, they could also invest and sometimes "gamble" their own depositor's savings. Pre-2008, banks were the most aggressive investors of mortgage-backed securities, utilizing aforementioned leverage strategies. Bear Sterns, formerly one of America's largest investment banks, borrowed $33 for every $1 of capital[36]. Where did the bulk of this newfound money go? You guessed, it mortgage-backed securities.

Today in the muddle of finance, it's difficult for the public to differentiate between the investment shop and the bank. Walk into Bank of America; boom a Merrill Lynch financial advisor greets you at the door. Dropping off a check at Wells Fargo, be prepared to speak with one of their highly acclaimed wealth managers. You would be hard pressed, even at the community bank level, not to be solicited for other financial services. One stop shop sounds ok on the cover, but I can't tell you how many clients I sit down with and ask them,

---

[36] "The End of a Wall Street Era, Even at Goldman Sachs", 09/28/2008, The New York Times

"Ok you have 90% of your portfolio in these IRA's with Citibank, elaborate on them."

Sweet old lady looks at me, "Well Bryan, we just rolled over all our retirement funds to the bank. You see me and Clarke are as conservative as they come, golly the thought of Las Vegas makes us sick. We're glad the bank was able to handle it for us though."

In turn I commend them on rolling over to an Individual Retirement Account to take advantage of their newfound control and flexibility. "That's great Miss, now where's the bank invest all that money."

"CD's Bryan. Certificates of Deposit are what my Dad did and his Dad before him." The poor elders don't even realize these charts that pepper their papers are riskier than they could have ever imagined. *But it's at the bank.* Times have changed; they are not simply CD's.

It's only recent history that you know what totally hit the fan. "The whole crisis came solely about our extravagant and vicious system of paper usury and bank credits, exciting people to wild speculation and gambling in stocks." Sounds like a perfect summary doesn't it? I'd say so, and so would the man who made that statement, President James Buchanan in 1856.

So how do we fix it when things go south? Well, if you owe the bank $1,000 and can't pay it, you have a problem. If you owe the bank $1,000,000 and can't pay it, they have a problem. This is when financial establishments become Too Big To Fail.

There may not be anything more frustrating to Main Street America than this notion of Too Big To Fail, or as I would say "Too Stupid To Kill." In essence, these morons got so powerful that we had to forgive them. Not only forgive them, but then give them more of our money. Like all the third graders going back to Joey and saying it's ok pal, here's another $100.

Like we mentioned in Step 3, economists call the result of this bail out mentality, "Moral Hazard"- when one party takes undue risk or irrational behavior because an event does not hold equal responsibility for all involved parties. In other words, I can screw up this time because you chumps will bail me out anyways.

I have a beautiful Rottweiler-Lab named Boomer. He was the funniest puppy, full of energy and always ready to tear the house down. I can recall coming home from work and kicking off my recently shined dress shoes, within a minute Boomer would fly by and grab a shoe. He'd run around the living room, slobbering and tearing my shoe. I would get up in a fury and run at him screaming, raise my hand in the air ready to smash him. He would immediately drop the shoe and cower in fear. With his cute puppy eyes, I could never bring myself to hit Boom. As time went on, Boomer kept grabbing my shoe, and I kept raising my hand. Eventually he could care less and kept on running around and eating my shoes. He knew I'd never actually hit him... America's largest institutions know we'll never hit them either.

Incentives can encourage one to do more of a good thing and less of a bad thing, but they don't arrive organically.

They come about from caring parents, teachers, cops, and sometimes politicians (more on this later).

***

It is fair to hypothesize that all aspects of life are dictated to some degree by economics. When you go out to lunch on Monday with your work buddies, after a bit of an excessive weekend, and opt for the free glass of water instead of the $2 Coke, that is an economic decision. When Democrats fight with Republicans how every person in America should pay more taxes, those are economic debates. Economics is the psychological study of money.

If you ask yourself the most basic questions of our lives- Why go to work today? Why choose one vacation versus the other? Why get divorced? Why take a long commute to the city job versus the local branch around the corner? Money, either consciously or subconsciously, touches each of these conversations.

Those same questions of the haves and have not's, the wants versus the needs, are faced by Fortune 500 organizations and policy makers around the globe. Read up on all the wars of our history and why they were provoked. Even back to the chapter quote by Thomas Jefferson... the USA is here today, yes because of a desire for independence, but the straw that broke the camel's back was money... Taxation without representation, on tea no less.

However, there are two sides to the economic coin, one is the mathematical rationale and the other is emotional inclination. For example, many financial advisors will tell their clients that the mortgage is the best kind of debt and masters of wealth should carry a mortgage throughout their entire lives. They go on to back up this recommendation via low fixed interest rates, smart leverage, tax deductions on mortgage interest, maintaining liquidity, and overall money in motion. Yet when I ask my clients what their biggest financial goals are at the onset of a financial planning arrangement, without fail "getting rid of the mortgage" falls in the top three.

I can run the numbers and show a myriad of scenarios with other debt reductions and investments and so on that in a certain instance that may not make sense. But to *them*, it makes sense. Emotion overcomes math.

In economic policy there are two distinct schools of thought: Capitalism and Socialism. They are polar opposites. Socialism has gained a negative connotation through communist governments that have oppressed their people and are often synonymous with the aforementioned dictatorships of Hitler, Soviet Union, North Korea, etc. Obviously the people who have abused this privilege are worse than the actual principles of socialism. Socialism is defined by the English World Dictionary as "an economic theory or system in which the means of production, distribution, and exchange are owned by the community collectively, usually through the state..."[37]

But make no mistake; I am a fan of pure capitalism. As Aristotle once said, "Wherever there's competition there's victory." Capitalism is competition. Priests say that the Lord helps those who help themselves. Welfare and socialism strip away this independent ambition. Capitalism focuses on

---

[37] "Socialism", English World Dictionary

enlarging the pie through competition, whereas Socialism focuses on reallocating the pie through intervention.

Even The Bible makes mention of God's favoritism towards the ideal of capitalism…

The Parable of the Bags of Gold
(Matthew 25:14-30 New International Version)

14: "Again, it will be like a man going on a journey, who called his servants and entrusted his wealth to them. 15: To one he gave five bags of gold, to another two bags, and to another one bag, [a] each according to his ability. Then he went on his journey. 16: The man who had received five bags of gold went at once and put his money to work and gained five bags more. 17: So also, the one with two bags of gold gained two more. 18 But the man who had received one bag went off, dug a hole in the ground and hid his master's money.

19: "After a long time the master of those servants returned and settled accounts with them. 20: The man who had received five bags of gold brought the other five. 'Master,' he said, 'you entrusted me with five bags of gold. See, I have gained five more.'

21: "His master replied, 'Well done, good and faithful servant! You have been faithful with a few things; I will put you in charge of many things. Come and share your master's happiness!'

22: "The man with two bags of gold also came. 'Master,' he said, 'you entrusted me with two bags of gold; see, I have gained two more.'

23: "His master replied, 'Well done, good and faithful servant! You have been faithful with a few things; I will put you in charge of many things. Come and share your master's happiness!'

24: "Then the man who had received one bag of gold came. 'Master,' he said, 'I knew that you are a hard man, harvesting where you have not sown and gathering where you have not scattered seed. 25: So I was afraid and went out and hid your gold in the ground. See, here is what belongs to you.'

26: "His master replied, 'You wicked, lazy servant! So you knew that I harvest where I have not sown and gather where I have not scattered seed? 27: Well then, you should have put my money on deposit with the bankers, so that when I returned I would have received it back with interest.

28: "'So take the bag of gold from him and give it to the one who has ten bags. 29: For whoever has will be given more, and they will have an abundance. Whoever does not have, even what they have will be taken from them. 30: And throw that worthless servant outside, into the darkness, where there will be weeping and gnashing of teeth.'

Personal financial decisions, both good and bad, bubble up to influence the largest of institutions and governments. In turn, these decision makers at the forefront lead the populace as each choice trickles down to our everyday lives. Such back and forth dictates economics. It may seem inconceivable at times, but proper financial planning can shelter your money in a way that leaves you in control and flexible to the constant actions and reactions of the financial world.

Step 10: Vote or Die

"Any city, however small is in fact divided into two, one for the poor, the other for the rich, they are at war with one another."
- Plato, The Republic

That single quote could not ring more true than it does today. The Pew Research Center points out that the gap between rich and poor is at an all-time high, with the median net worth of upper class families being about seven times that of middle-class families ($639,400 vs. $96,500)[38]. Such indicators subjugate the 24/7 media outlets that focus specifically on politics, each of them with their unabashed biases. It has become entertaining to listen to politicians on either side of the aisle communicate to each other like drunken baboons. As painful as it may seem, economic policy starts right here. And as insignificant as it may seem, your single vote guides the dialog. Choose wisely my friend.

The common man would rather put in ear plugs and flip the bird to politicians, but it's not so easy. Love em or hate em (it seems like most hate them), politicians are our representatives and they will speak on our behalf. Their decisions that go on in the hallowed halls of Capitol Hill, behind closed doors, dramatically affect us all.

It's a shame our society has become so engrossed by this procession as to not even really care. In the 2012 presidential election, amidst a heated contest with major issues at stake, amplified by more than $6 billion of advertising, only

---

[38] Pew Research- 2014

57.5% of eligible voters hit the booths[39]. Nearly half of America lacked the interest to get off their ass for five minutes and vote for how the country should be run. In 2004, P. Diddy rallied America with his "Vote or Die!" slogan, yet he too has since become a disenfranchised non-voter.

Recognize that every day you go to work a piece of your earnings, a substantial piece, will go to a charity not of your choosing. These tax dollars will be spread across the world in unfathomable arrangements. Modern politicians ought to recall a lesson from Luke 3:13 in which John The Baptist was asked by tax collectors, "Teacher, what shall we do?" And he replied to them, "Collect no more than your due from the people." That which the government gives it must first takeaway, and that huge transfer of wealth alone is not enough to appease Washington.

Debt can be a politician's best friend. It can buy him or her votes as it is funneled to the pork of promises previously made, provide immediate gratification through pet projects, or jolt the markets with an influx of cash. However, politicians come and go as the terms end or begin. Unfortunately, that debt will remain. Beware, a nation can be knotted in a snare of debt, and then their loyalty can be assured to its lender. Today there's over $19 trillion of American debt. And no one, I repeat NO one, has any idea how it will be repaid.

So how does a politician play both the game of garnering votes term to term, while at the same time curing the country's issues? President Harry Truman left office in 1953 with approval ratings in the twenties, awful! Today he is viewed as one of America's greatest presidents. Not only is politics a

[39] Center for The Study of The American Electorate

juggling act, but it's one that might not be fairly judged for decades down the road!

Present day can provide a perfect anecdote of how the results don't always add up to the rhetoric beforehand. Take for instance these two antonyms, a staunch Republican and a radical Democrat, Dubya vs. Obama.

Bush II is not only regularly ridiculed for prompting the Great Recession, but as a no holds barred Republican, he's an easy target for the Robin Hood wannabee's. As the figurehead for the GOP in 2000-2008, President Bush was tagged the classic "help the rich and screw the poor" conservative. Again, please don't merely take things at face value, but rather base opinions on empirical evidence.

One of the first movements of his presidency was The Bush Tax Cuts. Contrary to popular belief, once fully implemented these measures actually increased the portion of taxes on the wealthiest Americans. The top 1% of earners increased from 38.4% to 39.1% of the overall tax base, while the bottom 50% of Americans decreased from 3.4% to 3.1% of the overall tax base[40]. These tax cuts prevented a full recession after the Dot-Com bubble burst. Meanwhile the rate of unemployment averaged 5.3% during his presidency.

Bush's opposite, Barack Obama, proudly opposed Dubya across the board. Obama championed the working man, minorities, the poor, food stamps, and other liberal ideals. Outside of the not so "Affordable Care Act", which most critics currently consider a debacle, the most obvious success during his reign was the stock market. When Obama took office on

---

[40] Investors Business Daily, 11/30/2012

January 20, 2009, the DOW slumped to 7,949. At the writing of this book the DOW sits at about 17,000; up about 113% since his arrival. Do the working man, minorities, poor, and food stamp people lose sleep over the DOW? Actually it's the top tier of America with their fancy IRA's and 401(k)'s, or those hedge fund demons, who are reaping the benefit. Does this mean the rich Republicans owe Mr. Obama a thank you?

Cause and effect, man's natural yearning for finding patterns in life, can only be clouded by politics. Put the survival of the fittest Republicans against the caring, tax and share Democrats aside for a moment. One thing everyone can agree on is blaming President George W. Bush for the real estate collapse right?

In 2003 President Bush proposed a regulation bill to address the real estate markets. Democratic Senator Barney Frank promptly replied, Fannie Mae and Freddie Mac were doing fine. After seventeen more regulation proposals brought to the floor by George W. Bush, and five more years, 2008 happened. Now if we look back at recent history and this Great Recession, the public generally would point out Dubya as the scapegoat. But was it entirely his fault? Or were the wheels set in motion long before?

The collision of politics and economics can often be routed back to the management of banking. In 2008, banks were allowed to use leverage and aggressively invest in mortgage backed securities thanks to the previously mentioned Graham-Leach-Bliley Act. This is the most commonly pointed out reason for the real estate collapse on the Bush Administration's watch. Yet it was during Bill Clinton's presidency, with the guidance of Treasury Secretary Robert

Rubin, that these deregulation acts were passed (Rubin conveniently then jumped to Citigroup).

Many will blame predatory lending by banks for the 2008 fiasco, mortgage bankers trying to make an easy commission on some No Doc loan. This free for all was OK'd and then embraced by politicians. They may have marketed it as the feel good story that every American could own a home, but we all know the outcome. As Ben Franklin said centuries ago when asked about social engineering, "Whenever we attempt to mend the scheme of providence, we had need be very circumspect lest we do more harm than good."

Even further back in time to 1979... South Dakota became the first state to repeal usury laws. In 1981 Citibank immediately set up shop in South Dakota to exploit this law via credit cards. Now credit cards are the most profitable segment of the entire banking industry.

So here we are today, and the changes happening month by month before our eyes are sweeping; some even challenging our own Constitution. You may still be asking how one of the most radical presidents, Obama, made it to the White House. We've seen the economic reasoning in the previous chapter, but take a look at this...

In 1860 William Seward was upset in one of the most unexpected Presidential elections of that time. A lawyer from Illinois shocked the world. When asked how this lanky fellow from the middle of nowhere won the nation's votes, Seward said, "The leader of a political party in a country like ours is so exposed that his enemies become as numerous and formidable as his friends... Lincoln was comparatively unknown, had not to contend with the animosities generally marshaled against a leader." Perhaps this small reasoning of history could be applied to today, and the meteoric rise of President Barack Obama. The public loves drama, gossip, and a pissing contest on the biggest of stages. Like Seward alluded, a politician with a clean slate might actually have a leg up on a successful man who's lived under the microscope for so long.

In our parent's generation there were a handful of channels to come home to, and one influential voice in Walter Cronkite. Conspiracy theorists then feared that there might be a lack of information on which to base political opinion. In a polar opposite scenario, today presents such a plethora of information that stations align themselves with a congruent message. Viewers are more sheltered now than then as we gravitate towards a channel that meets our already existing predispositions.

This book should not become another platform for political debate. The purpose here is to enlighten and empower millennials to make sound financial decisions. So in closing, Harry Truman once said, "The only thing new in the world is the history you don't know." So please pay attention to what's come before us, and cast your ballot. To click the button or not click the button is your personal decision to be Responsible- the cause of a matter, or to be the Victim- the effect of a matter.

Step 11: Win at Work

"By faithfully working eight hours a day you may one day get to be a boss and work twelve hours a day."- Robert Frost

Not long ago, I was catching up with one of my best friends over an incredible enchilada at the one and only Jose Tejas. In spite of being financial advisors at rival companies, we are like shrinks to one another. We played football in college together, and ever since he's been my partner in crime. This one time all-night party animal is now a proud, and exhausted, parent. I asked him what the biggest change was since becoming a daddy. He made a comment I didn't see coming from a cocky and ultra-competitive personality, "You know something I've realized, in our business you can work to make a lot of money; or you can work to make a lot of spare time."

I spend my life talking to my clients about becoming financially independent. It's a term that's thrown around our industry, but few really know what it means. I always thought financial independence meant living on your own. It's taken a long time for me to understand it, and financial independence might not even be the best term for what we're trying to get across, but ultimately it's freeing your thoughts from the interruption of money.

As Sir Francis Bacon once said, "Money makes a good servant, but a bad master." Most people let money be their master, rather than declare their independence and achieve financial freedom (the other catchphrase). People come in all different shapes and sizes, so do our tastes for lifestyle and luxury. There are clients who envision retirement as a hike through the park followed by a fresh sandwich picnic; and others who dream of sailing the world and eating caviar by the bucket load. Money is irrelevant at the end of the day; it's all about what you do, when you do, and with whom. Only you can determine what financial independence means.

The first step to financial liberation is working where you want to work, not where you have to. Gallup conducted a worldwide poll in 189 countries that showed only 13.3% of workers liked their job[41]. Prosperous people agree that money is only a byproduct of winning. Winning at what they love is the true goal.

If you find yourself asking what job you love, look no further than your passions. If you find yourself asking what your passions are, look no further than what excites you. Excitement is the biological synonym of passion and happiness, it's a cure all. When you find boredom, run! Positive anticipation is the spoon that stirs your fruit loops.

If you're confused on what excites you, look no further than your curiosities. The fear of death is caused solely by unsatisfied curiosities. Self-help books abound implore that your Sundays should feel like Fridays, from the exhilaration of the week to come! That might be a little excessive, but it drives home the point that the workweek is where most hours are spent, and it should be looked forward to. Excitement is when you're already planning out your goals for the day on your drive in, rather than drifting off to the music and saying to yourself, "Make it another nine hours and Monday will be done." If you

---

[41] "Worldwide, 13% of Employees are Engaged at Work", Gallup- 10/08/2013

are not enjoying the journey of a career, then what the hell is the point of the money anyways?

When I interview a candidate, I often bring up what I call the "three I's". The three I's stand for Income, Independence, and Impact...

To the point of impact, Masonic luminary Albert Pike once said, "What we have done for ourselves alone dies with us; what we have done for others in the world remains and is immortal." Or as Booker T. Washington famously said, "If you want to lift yourself up, lift someone else up." This missing component is regularly found in behind the scenes positions, such as the analyst. The employee who works his own schedule and makes high six figures, but halfway through life implodes crying, "All I ever see is this computer screen and I don't know what's the point of it all!?"

Independence goes back to working where and when you want. Is it a job in which you can still coach your son's soccer game? Or is it a job in which you'll be traveling the world and forgetting what grade your kids are in? "Thanks for your tireless service the past twenty years Mr. Employee, but we're relocating headquarters and you'll be moving out to Idaho in February." This is routine for the Big Four Accounting firms; ambitious college grads proudly take their staff job only to lose their twenties to eighty hour work weeks.

Finally there is income, unfortunately countless individuals love where they work and feel it's a worthy profession, but they are forced out of a career because the income won't match their lifestyle. Financial planning can keep more of these happy workers right where they are. This seed of discontent is often found in teachers and cops for example.

Fulfilled people all share a similar path. I've asked and researched these guys that walk on water about what separated them from the pack and launched their careers. The common impetus is exactly that, they separated themselves from the pack. It's imperative to stop the zombie walk found in the rat race and take a step back. As professionals say, "Stop working in your practice and take a second to work on your practice." It is astonishing how in that a moment of calm you can achieve an AHA moment, a small tweak to your work that fixes all the bugs. The right blend of emotional control and momentum can allow the mind to run wild. Lao-Tsu once said, "To the mind that is still the whole universe surrenders." Like Michael Jordan peacefully preparing to nail a free throw in front of 20,000 screaming fans. If you still seem stuck on the hamster wheel and unable to come up with a new solution, try yoga!

The magic that keeps any productive worker going is momentum. It can devastate us or carry us far beyond our wildest dreams. Momentum is the Emotion Multiplier. However, like any emotion, it can be a positive or a negative.

The only way to maintain the positive energy is to keep on working. "Life is like riding a bicycle. To keep your balance you must keep moving." Albert Einstein said that. In a small business that means a never-ending quest for innovation and customer acquisition. If either stops for a second, you will fall off.

When momentum becomes obsession, the effects can be as harmful as they may be helpful. This realization provoked me to ask several of my colleagues at a conference what they would do if they closed their "case of the year". The answers... go on a cruise, fly out to Vegas, or treat my girlfriend to a long weekend. Ok we're on the same page I thought. But the top producer in our company defiantly said- work some more. That time when we are on Cloud Nine is when we're at our best, you're on the heater, make the tough phone call, and schedule your biggest client. Taking off then would be like LeBron James sinking back-to-back 3's with the game on the line and then asking the coach to take him out.

So when should you take that vacation to Fiji? At the point in time where you feel like nothing's going right. This might sound like throwing in the towel, opposed to a winner's hymn of when things get tough the tough get going. The concept of R&R is one of hardest for successful people to grasp. That feeling that we'll miss a week as our competitors blow right by us. A stop at nothing attitude is crucial to long-term success, but recharge the batteries when they're empty, not full. Plus, your customers may think less of you if they're seeing their vendor talk like a dreary eyed mope.

Another great way to stimulate momentum is to analyze strengths and weaknesses. Good companies find the flaw in the mirror and try to cover it up. Contrarily, rejecting perfection may be half the battle towards happiness. As Neils Bohr once said, "An expert is someone who's made all the mistakes that can be made in a very narrow field."

Great companies also try to make their weaknesses good, but they try much harder to make their strengths great! It is our talents that really separate us. Have you ever seen a Cy Young winning pitcher also bat for .300? Act like the pro's do and exploit your gifts. It makes one feel better about oneself and increases the Money/Emotion Multiplier... momentum!

***

By this point, you've learned to find a job you love, how to move up in your company, and create a work-life balance. If you feel like you're taking all the necessary steps, but are still stuck in a rut, then it may be time for you to be the maker of change. The best way to blaze your own trail is to be a leader.

Entrepreneurship it is the backbone of the American economy. It is an opportunity to take newfound ideas and make them an economic generator.

The first step to become a leader is to step out of your comfort zone. Entrepreneurs should strive to take on at least one uncomfortable task each day. If you are not encountering decisions that make you think twice, you're at a standstill. The bigger decisions are known as *Pussy Junction*. This is the famous crossroads at which you decide to make the big call, speak up at the annual meeting, or approach the hot chick at the end of the bar. Champions have all been there, and for the movers and shakers, on a more regular basis. That decision to step up to the plate or stay on the bench dictates the path of life. If you reflect on where you are and who surrounds you, it all stems from a series of consequences over which you originally had no control. The choices you make in light of them are what guide your life. So, make it a goal to drive to *Pussy Junction* on a daily basis, and when you get there make the turn you know is right.

Such advice probably sounds intimidating to someone unfamiliar with being the owner of a business or face of an organization. You may harbor feelings of "I'm not ready yet, and I'm putting on a front to hold down this position." That's normal, we all have to start somewhere. The key to profitability is not letting people know when that starting point actually is.

There's a famous scene in Boiler Room in which Ben Affleck tells his rookie stock brokers that they must "Act As If". Or as I mentioned earlier in regards to networking, fake it until you make it. Herminia Abarra captured this perfectly in her Harvard Business Review article, "The Authenticity Paradox". When we are thrust into a new position we often feel like impostors going against our natural inclinations. This excuse forces us back to what's comfortable and disables us from inspiring followers. To learn we must adopt unnatural and superficial behaviors. Being a chameleon to the situation can buy time until our skills have developed to match the new role. So don't be afraid to bite off more than you can chew, and if your narrative stretches a bit further than who you are, don't feel like a fraud but rather a forerunner.

My first marketing teacher, and high school football coach, used to say that losers' lives are full of shoulda, coulda, woulda's. "They shoulda shoulda shoulda... before you know it they shoulda all over themselves." You can't build success on just on what you *intend* to do.

The most popular flaw for entrepreneurs is entrepreneuritis, an attitude to try and do it all. Be careful as it's possible to be overwhelmed by opportunities the same as to starve from too little.

I recommend for young entrepreneurs, or any leader for that matter, to study John Maxwell's Five Levels of Leadership. The first leadership position is precisely that, one of "Position". This is the manager; they are there simply because someone put them there. People are following them because they have to. There can be wonderful managers, and there can be terrible managers. A poor manager is the boss who never sets an example and fails to connect with his team, instead he sits atop his make believe throne to say "I am the boss!" As the old saying goes, "If you think you are leading but look behind and see no one following, you're just taking a walk". When you need help in your organization, seek talent not title.

Maxwell's second step in leadership is "Permission". This is the point when you not only hold a title as a supervisor, but actually have followers. Solid relationships are built on this level, and now people are following you because they want to. This isn't to say you are the best leader or living the dream life, but the foundation is in place as the recognized leader. You are a captain not only in name, but also in the minds of employees.

The third rung of leadership is "Production". This is when the rubber meets the road. Now you not only have the title, but your employees want to follow you, and they look up to your results. The proof is in the pudding, there is no substitute for performance. "Production" is the element that makes your team go from a group of friends to a winning unit.

The fourth level of leadership is "People Development". Leaders who attain this level are the cream of the crop. Transitioning from Level Three to Level Four may be the hardest, because it requires a premier producer who's finally reached the zenith to then only forfeit some of that production in exchange for coaching. Companies or producers' end results decline during this transition as their efforts are rerouted, but if done correctly the future increases can be exponential. The sign you've made it here is when one of your longstanding employees comes to you and says, "Thanks boss for the opportunity and all you've done for me." Your employees are not only efficient cogs in the machine, but they are devotees for your cause. In building an organization, recruit motivated people, don't motivate recruited people. The Level Four Leader attracts this sort of talent.

Maxwell's last level of leadership is "Pinnacle". Reaching this status is reserved for the elite. This is another phase that truly forces a leader out of their comfort zone, as it requires a relinquishing of lifelong control to your newly developed captains. Marines hate to be called a micromanager or control freak by subordinates. If an officer tells his platoon to add up to four, he should not care if they used 1+3 or 2+2, as long as the mission was accomplished. At this point you've essentially become an ideal that people strive to mimic. You are a mini living legend at this stage. The business community respects your organization and a reputation has been achieved that has a life of its own. Flourishing business owners will brag that they, "couldn't blow their business up if they wanted to". That's the Pinnacle Level.

Having a dedicated team with a captain leading the way is all well and good, but the foundation of gainful entrepreneurship has to be an idea. Ever think of the paper clip? What about the staple? Or better yet, the Post-It? Of course we all could have come up with that, how did we not think of that sooner! Discovery is about seeing what others see, but thinking what others do not. There were mobs of people spilling papers across every desk in America until Samuel B. Fay used a clip to attach paper to fabric and sought a patent in 1867.

Business of all sizes, from the one man law firm to Google, are all searching for that perfect idea. Coming up with the idea is only the first step. Trying to perfect the product so it fits society like a glove is what makes a winner. The process of achievement must not be imitated, but it has to be duplicated. In other words, create a product or service that's unique to you, with systems in place to do so consistently. The only thing worse than outright failure is achieving that success you've longed for, but without total understanding of how it was done.

Financial planning and an efficient government are great, but you are the engine that makes the whole thing move. Be bold and attack whatever your visions may be. Failure is the quickest way to success, so fail fast and move on. Michael Jordan missed more than 9,000 shots in his career; lost almost 300 games; and 26 times missed the game winning shot. The greatest of all time will be the first to tell you that repeated failures are the path to success.

Step 12: Retire Tomorrow

*"Musicians don't retire; they stop when there's
no more music in them." - Louis Armstrong*

After a long, successful career there is only one more stop... retirement. A long time ago people didn't retire, they died. Shortly thereafter, they didn't retire, they moved from working outside to working inside. According to The Federal Reserve, the number of years spent in leisure, time off, and retirement rose from 11 years in 1870 to 35 years in 1990. On the same subject, The Fed reports that Americans worked 66 hours per week in 1850, 51 hours in 1909, and 34.8 hours currently[42]. Today it seems our purpose of work is to stop working, virtually half of our life can be spent on sabbatical. There's obviously been a huge transformation in the word retirement, and its effects are rippling across the country.

If you flip back to the beginning of this book, you'll recall that Social Security is the largest source of Retiree Income. Coming in second are Defined Benefit Pensions. Both of these systems are facing severe challenges. As population dynamics shift to more retirees and less workers, with retirement checks frequently lasting as long as paychecks, young professionals should not be so certain of this form of income.

Most millennials will be left with that defined contribution option- 401(k) or Individual Retirement Arrangement. This book discusses all sorts of bailouts- bail outs

---

[42] "50 Reasons We're Living Through The Greatest Period in World History", Morgan Housel, Motley Fool- 2014

of banks, huge financial institutions, even IOU's to keep those lofty pensions going. There is one plan the government will not bail out, the 401(k) or IRA you built with your own hard earned money. The Federal Reserve reported in 2011 that IRA's held about $4.87 trillion and 401(k)'s totaled $3.88 trillion! You can rest assured those numbers are even larger now with recent bull markets. Not only are you 100% responsible for their performance, with no government subsidy when markets tank, but financial experts agree that politicians on both sides are foaming at the mouth for all those looming tax dollars.

The vehicles we use to get us to retirement are one thing, but how we drive them on the home stretch is the real test. Look at it this way, imagine you are Dale Earnhardt Jr. and you're revving your engine to start the Daytona 500. Right as the race is to begin, you glance up at the leaderboard and notice that today's race will only be a 50 lap sprint. Wait a minute! I thought this was the Daytona 500 and they immediately changed the race of a lifetime to fifty laps?

Next year you step into your race car prepared to race 500 miles like it's supposed to be. Only the race official mentions at the last moment that this year's Daytona 500 will be a Le Mans style 2,000 laps! What the heck!?

This same ambiguity is found in retirement. One day you'll have prepared all those years, only to approach the starting line with no idea if it's time to drive for 50 laps or 2,000. And to make it a little more fun, the race officials (Uncle Sam) are going to change the rules throughout the race. Now that makes preparation pretty difficult, doesn't it?

Most of the pie chart people today (financial advisors) focus strictly on accumulation. "You see Mr. Smith, if you invest

X amount with me every year for the next Y years of your career and get Z rate of return, you'll end up with all this money. It's simple." Yah but then what Mr. Pie chart? "Well then I retire and you figure the rest out."

The distribution phase is the back nine, and any good golfer knows that wins are made in crunch time. Most financial planning literature recommends individuals be able to replace 70-80% of their pre-retiree income. Bear in mind, US life expectancy at birth in 1800 was 39 years, 49 years in 1900, 68 years in 1950, and 79 years today[43]. That back nine has changed from a bargain chip n putt to an expensive par five.

There are a number of key steps in a distribution strategy to combat this uncertainty:

1. **Time distributions to avoid penalties, taxes and down markets.**

How is that possible? Don't lump your entire life's savings into one pie chart; instead bucket your money. A widespread fault in retirement planning is that all the assets are commingled without purpose. Remember that investment triangle? Manage your liquidity, this way you don't have to make snap decisions and pay early withdrawal penalties, or even worse miss RMD's (Required Minimum Distributions) or take excess withdrawals on your annuity/pension. If you hedge your future tax liabilities, including a balance of Taxable, Tax-Deferred, and Tax-Free (preferably more of this) monies, then you'll consequentially have much more flexibility. Last of all, don't build a proper asset allocation and then sit there. That's

---

[43] "50 Reasons We're Living Through The Greatest Period in World History", Morgan Housel, Motley Fool- 2014

like buying perfectly fitted TaylorMade's and then leaving them in the basement. Design a distribution strategy so that equities can be liquidated at all-time highs and fixed income/cash stays available after correction years.

2. Insure your Retirement.

To take our bucket strategy a step further, do not neglect the afterlife. That's right, the days when you're no longer here. The most efficient way to transfer wealth, bar none, is via Life Insurance. If you have the foresight to purchase a permanent life insurance policy, preferably Whole Life, you can purchase dollars for pennies. A respectable rate of return will also be shielded from income taxes, and even estate taxes (if structured properly). With this huge reserve in the back pocket, you then have a permission slip to spend your retirement funds and never disinherit your loved ones. Beneficiaries will be able to pay all those awful income and estate taxes due on your IRA's with the insurance proceeds, so that the IRA funds are realized in whole. The kids are happy, and the parents are free to spend as they please!

3. Stretch your IRA.

Have you ever met anyone that distributed their entire IRA in just one year? I have, they're called kids. Clients trudge through decades of retirement, giving their all to defer taxes and keep that IRA growing (so afraid to touch that "expensive" money as my one client says). They navigate all those years to coddle this IRA as if it's a baby that can't be spoiled, only to one day die and pass it on to the kids. Then what? "Wow we got this $500k from my Mom and Pop? Time to get that new house on the hill we've been dreaming of" After decades of careful oversight, in only a few days that entire nest egg is liquidated.

Uncle Sam's wet dream, a huge tax due in an artificially high tax bracket!

4. Take advantage of The Gift of The Century- Roth IRA

The Individual Retirement Arrangement (IRA) was conceived in 1975, and its prettier sister, Roth, has only been around since 1997. The Taxpayer Relief Act of 1997 gave birth to this beauty. Direct contributions go in Post-Tax (no deduction this year), grow Tax-Free and are accessible Tax-Free (if held for five years and until 59 ½), no matter how large they've grown! Those same contributions, the money you put in, are also accessible to you at any point both tax and penalty free. And those Required Minimum Distributions you find so annoying in your senior years, not applicable here. So, instead of paying a huge tax bill on all the harvest, you're paying a little tax bill on the tiny seedlings.

Now the Roth isn't for everyone, the lovely US government says that if you work too hard and make too much money, you're no longer allowed to dance with Roth (2016- $117k filing single and $184k filing jointly). However, if you have one of those big pre-tax IRA's and are afraid of being punished down the road, you can pay the current tax owed and convert to a Roth IRA (no income limits for such a conversion). Let me share a trade secret I personally use- if your income exceeds the aforementioned limits, you can still make a non-deductible IRA contribution and immediately convert this to a Roth IRA... voila a "Backdoor Roth IRA"! Fortunately, more and more companies today are adopting the Roth 401(k). This works about the same way, except there are no income restrictions! That's correct, tax-free growth for even you Mister Highly Compensated Employee.

This is a good opportunity to bring back our close friends, the CPA's (Certified Public Accountants). If you walk into any accounting firm's lobby, you'll notice one of the key bullets in their little company brochure... Max out your 401(k) and IRA contributions. It's a blanket recommendation that's blasted at us ad nausea. Why the love affair?

Quick vignette... I was called into a meeting with some extremely wealthy clients and their accountants to discuss group disability insurance. The CPA firm made it a policy to have all of their executives and employees fund Group Disability Insurance on a Pre-Tax basis. I interrupted, "Wait, so when you're healthy and working, you want a little break. But when you're sick, out of work, and there's no income to speak of, then you want to pay the big tax bill." My clients quickly sided with me. After the meeting I politely confronted the CPA, Patrick. He sheepishly replied, "Listen Bryan, as a CPA we're taught from day one that you defer, defer, defer... take every break the IRS gives us, and then worry about the rest later." Patrick, I'd like to enjoy every candy bar I see, but someday I'll be fat and decrepit. Sometimes it pays to swallow your medicine today and enjoy a tax-free tomorrow.

There are also trappings that go along with the CPA's beloved qualified plan. The most common one is the RMD, Required Minimum Distribution. There are countless strategies to avoid having to take out your money and pay the tax man. You read that right, professionals like me spend hours consulting with clients to scheme how NOT to use your money.

Elderly folks go so far as to take Home Equity Lines of Credit and Reverse Mortgages just to live. Are they broke? Nope, they're millionaires. These clients have a fortune stashed away in IRAs, but bring up the idea of using Retirement funds in retirement and they begin to turn green and shake. "I will use every feasible source of money before touching that tax ploy, I'm not going to give in to Uncle Sam for all that money I earned and invested. No way!"

There simply isn't a more convoluted vehicle than the qualified plan. Those tax codes mean that you have an investment partner. His name is government, and he gets to call the shots every step of the way.

**

Now that you have a better understanding of how long retirement may last and the different vehicles that can drive you there, let's take a look at what might derail even the best of plans. The three biggest threats to retirement are- market volatility, taxes, and most of all healthcare. Many people spend their health chasing wealth, only to then spend that wealth in an attempt to regain health.

The sad reality is that we will either die suddenly, or become 100% dependent on another person. Longtermcare.gov cited in 2010 that over 70% of people over age 65 will require Long Term Care[44]. *Did I mention that it's kind of expensive?*

Healthcare is the fastest growing segment of the federal budget. America's health spending has doubled from around 7.5% of GDP in 1972 to more than 18% in 2015, and is projected to reach 34% in 2040[45]! People are quick to appoint

---

[44] Longtermcare.gov
[45] "The Economic Case for Healthcare Reform", WhiteHouse.gov

Medicare/Medicaid as our savior. President Johnson created Medicare in 1965, and it has been a topic of controversy ever since.

The government is usually not the most efficient director of funds. For instance, private insurers added Mammogram coverage to protect against breast cancer; it took Medicare more than ten years and an act of Congress to get up to speed.

There have been some improvements during the past couple of decades. But as with anything in government, trying to make a change is like doing an about-face with a cruise liner. One of the most impactful motions happened on December 8, 2003 when President George Bush signed the Medicare Modernization Act. This new law added a prescription drug plan to Medicare, created HSA's, and injected competition into Medicare.

Medicare is not only playing a constant game of catchup, it's also broke. The combination of rising health-care costs and the upcoming retirement of the baby boomer generation has created a $36.8 trillion unfunded liability[46]. The next generation (mine) will eat this bill.

The best part of retirement today is that it's longer than ever. The worst part of retirement today is that it's longer than ever. Your first day on the job feels like yesterday, which means retirement will feel like tomorrow. So start planning now, and remember that it's never too late to start.

---

[46] "2015 Medicare/Social Security Trustees' Report Analysis"

Step 13: Master The Comeback

"The best time to plant a shade tree was 25 years ago. If you haven't done so, the 2nd best time is now."
-Chinese Proverb

Here are a number of famous names, if you know what they all have in common, you'll get a prize:

Taylor Barnum, Henry John Heinz, Frank Baum, Mark Twain, Henry Ford, Walt Disney, Milton Suavely Hershey, Donald Trump, Larry King, Charles Goodyear, and Wayne Newton… Keep them in mind throughout this chapter.

Have you ever tried driving while looking in the rear view mirror? It's not easy, frankly if you did it for more than a few moments you'll probably total your car. Yet when it comes to money, that's what people do. Cling to that one great investment, or wail over that one lousy advisor. Look towards the future and prepare for tomorrow, not yesterday.

Once you pass fifty, you should never pass a bathroom, never trust a fart, and never think financial planning is out of reach. Regardless of your age, I encourage you to take a hard look at where your financial life is. If you're happy, that's great, if you're not, maybe it's time for a change. Do what you've done and be what you've been.

Starting late is never easy, but better late than never. This sad syndrome is found repeatedly amongst cigarette smokers. They figure they've been puffing away for the past forty years, so why stop now? As medical professionals will agree, quitting smoking even up to your senior years can have an immeasurable impact on your health. The same applies for finance. If you've got yourself into a bit of a hole, don't keep digging, man up and climb out.

Even if you're on the back nine, it's ok to change course. I've had plenty of meetings with senior citizens in which I bring up a recommendation contrary to what they've done their entire life. As they vehemently defend their past errors, it begins to feel like the "You can't handle the truth!" scene from A Few Good Men.

Sometimes you can't teach an old dog new tricks. It's upsetting to meet someone with such an ego that can stare straight at a mistake and say "Bry I know what you mean, but I've been doing it this way for forty years. I hate change." The best salesmen will swallow his pride and let the client down softly with the old, "It may have been right then, but maybe there's a chance to improve all the magnificent work you've done on your own thus far." Clients create objections based on either the fear of impaired control, or the fear of impaired income. The former is much harder to rebut than the latter.

If you are ready to join the party, your first step should be to calculate your balance sheet- assets and liabilities. Once these items are accounted for, create a detailed budget. WARNING- if you feel behind schedule after this checkup, do NOT fall into the trap of playing catch up with your portfolio. It's time to get aggressive with your saving, not with your allocation. Countless plans go from bad to worse with this "double down" mentality. Once your strategy is up to date, it's important to make some realistic choices of what's doable in retirement- the wants versus the needs. From here, turn over the new leaf and put your adjustments into action.

As for those superstars of entertainment and business mentioned earlier, they've all gone through the humbling process known as bankruptcy. If they could climb back from literally being broke and go onto such heights, you can start planning and salvage your retirement. Like William James once said, "One of the greatest discoveries of my generation is that human beings can alter their lives by altering their attitudes of mind." In other words, change the way you look at things and the things you look at will change.

Step 14: Pack a Swiss Army Knife

"Companion For Life" - Victorinox

In 1891 Karl Elsener, with help from 27 other cutler makers, filled a huge military order for a standard issue knife and his original soldier's knife (four other components). Elsener then named his company Victorinox, after his mom Victoria.

Several decades later in World War II, we Yankees made the knife famous. American soldiers fell in love with the tool they coined, The Swiss Army Knife. Today there are in excess of 350 different models of Swiss Army Knife, with Victorinox producing close to 3.6 million knives per month.

What's important about this silly little knife with spoons, forks, and corkscrews? Well, it's a life-saver in so many situations. It's a tool with multiple uses that can address daily aspects across your whole life.

I'm often asked what kind of silver bullet can mimic this Swiss Army Knife in the world of money- a tool that can protect you, your family, your business, and life savings. Whole Life! Its name pretty much sums it up; Whole Life Insurance has complimented each stage of life for centuries. It is unquestionably the Swiss Army Knife of finance.

One of the top advisors in the country likes to call it "The Pope Mobile." You ever notice how the Pope comes to America and cruises around in his glass bubble? He rides through the streets of New York City, people can be killing each other, robbing stores, lighting trash cans on fire, and drinking out of paper bags, yet the Pope keeps smiling and waving.

The goal of a financial planner is to put you in the Pope mobile. The markets tank, interest rates spike, inflation erodes your dollar, taxes go through the roof, you die in a safari accident, you can't work after losing your arm trying the Home Depot Do It Yourself saw, you start to drool on yourself and require Long Term Care... Each of these scenarios could completely ruin a financial plan. What is one financial vehicle that is sheltered from all of these trepidations? You guessed it- Whole Life!

F.A. Hayek, winner of the Nobel Prize, stated that savings through Cash Value Life Insurance and one's home are the most important investments you can make. One of them you can actually live and raise a family in while investing in it. The other can save your family while generating a tax-free dividend. Whole Life Insurance is private property; I challenge you to think of another investment protected from interruption of tax law, market risk, withdrawal penalties, sickness or injury, death, job changes, inflation, and the like. Permanent life insurance is a unique instrument that in nearly every Retirement Planning scenario can allow the same legacy with greater cash flow, or a greater legacy with the same cash flow.

Why has Whole Life Insurance withstood the test of time? The George Washington Bridge was made to withstand tractor trailers bumper to bumper on both levels in the middle of a hurricane. If you pass over the bridge all by yourself in a coupe at 3:00AM, does the GW reward you with a refunded toll for being the only car? Not to my knowledge. Whole Life was designed with the same worst-case scenario in mind, however when over-engineering is present in a favorable economy, these companies reward their drivers in the form of a dividend!

Another huge fan of insurance is Warren Buffett. He's mentioned several times throughout the course of his career the rare capabilities of insurance companies. He takes maximum advantage of cash and liquidity through their "Float". This is the premiums insurance companies hold onto for long periods of time before ever having to pay out a claim. Buffett credits this concept as to why insurance companies can be so profitable.

One more case study you may be familiar with is the happiest place on earth. Walt Disney used a $100,000 loan from his life insurance policy to start Walt Disney Inc. and build Disneyland. After his bankruptcy, animators and studios walked out on him. With little collateral and inability to acquire lending, his Whole Life policy provided much needed capital.

If some of these brilliant minds aren't enough to get you thinking, take a look at the stewards of all our money... banks. As revealed earlier, banks must hold a certain amount of reserves. These assets are qualified by "Tiers", Tier 1 Capital being the safest form. In 2014, banks owned $149.6 billion of Cash Value Life Insurance[47]. These monster institutions take full advantage of cash value life insurance for the same reasons small businesses and wealthy families do.

Banks, endowment funds, and other institutions actually like this vehicle so much they changed the way the game was played. In the 1980's the IRS had enough of this "misuse" of Life Insurance and created the Modified Endowment Contract. This act was in retaliation to such institutions using Cash Value as a tax shelter with a nice rate or

---

[47] Equias Alliance/Michael White Bank Owned Life Insurance (BOLI) Holdings Report

return. The MEC is a rule that governs the growth of cash value in an insurance policy, forcing it to be taxed like an investment when funded in the wrong manner.

Believe it or not the main competitor to Whole Life is Term Insurance. This is sort of like saying the biggest competition for that house you want to buy is the apartment down the street. Does it sound like you're comparing apples and oranges? Consumers don't recognize this when they get caught up in a sales pitch.

If there was a 1% chance of rain tomorrow, would you carry an umbrella? Uh no. If the weatherman said there was going to be a 100% chance of rain- it's glued to your hip. Studies show that term insurance pays a death claim approximately 1% of the time. Say you're taking a flight out of LaGuardia Airport and the guy at the gate says, "You can park in Lot A and it will cost you $20 per day for your seven day trip. Or you can park in Lot B which will cost you $100 per day, but when you return from vacation we'll give you back your $700 plus interest." Which lot would you pick? *For full disclosure, I sell plenty of Term Insurance too, it's a vital product for providing huge, temporary layers of protection at an affordable cost to those with budgetary constraints. But, it should not be used as a one or the other approach versus Permanent Life Insurance.*

After determining which type of life insurance you want, you must examine the best companies for the job. In the industry there are essentially two kinds- Mutuals and Stockhelds. Mutual companies are 100% owned by their policyholders. That means there are no shareholders to satisfy with quarterly earnings or dividends demanded. The owner of a stockheld policy does not receive his/her dividends until all shareholders have been paid. If you were to look at the Comdex rankings of all major carriers, you'll notice the few mutuals stand above the hundreds of stockhelds. Remember; do not shop for bargains in Life Insurance, parachutes, or toilet paper. You do NOT want any of them to fall apart.

In spite of the population of America being double what it was in 1940, less Life Insurance is actually being purchased today. In 2015, life insurance ranked seventh among financial priorities with 43% of Americans admitting to no coverage at all[48]! Have we become a cheaper nation? A more selfish nation? Or perhaps a misguided one?

"Life Insurance has to do with the most sacred things that stir the human affections... Its management involves a higher duty and more constant devotion than we associate with a mere business enterprise." These words were spoken by President Grover Cleveland in 1905. His advice serves as a testament to the need for financial professionals, rather than confused customers shopping for the best sale.

---

[48] 2015 Insurance Barometer Study

Step 15: No Excuses

*"In all things, success depends upon previous preparation, and
without such preparation, there is to be such failure."*
- Confucius

I've heard every excuse in the book on why NOT to plan.
I'll tell you the unequivocal Top Three in a minute. But first
there are a few common ones that shouldn't be left out...

"Financial Planning? That's for rich people!"- You are
rich dummy. I hear this one so often from solid professionals
who make six figures. What the hell are you waiting for?! Sure
financial planners would love to work only with people making
millions a year, but if that were the case we'd all be sitting
around scratching our heads. If you really don't think you are
rich, why don't you start preparing to be rich? You deserve it!

Outside of that humble crowd, there are your old Do It
Yourselfers. Lots of times these guys are engineers, introverts,
people who might have been "burned", or your classic know it
all. Scientists once believed the Earth was flat, not because they
were ignorant, but rather the appearance of knowledge wrongly
confirmed a falsehood. As stated previously, the smartest
people are those who can admit what they don't know. Unless
you stayed at a Holiday Inn last night, there are certain subjects
that should receive a specialist's advice.

Seinfeld has an awesome parody on this demographic.
The dude who watches HGTV, runs out to Home Depot, buys
the "arm chopper saw" and "destroy your walls nail gun", then
comes home to wreak havoc. Don't waste thousands of dollars

and a year of work when a professional can knock it out lickety split, that's why they're there.

The other excuse I get is the Great Recession. The media loves the hype of fear and negativity. The recent recession provided an enormous crutch and once in a lifetime opening for losers to say "Everyone has it tough right now, and I don't know if I'll ever get a job or make money again. But hey at least we're all in the same boat". Bologna! Winners know that recessions have opportunity written all over them. Downturns produce discounted infrastructure, bargain freelancers, and cheap advertising. Buy when things are on sale rather than at a premium, so stop complaining.

Without further ado, the Top Three Reasons why the rest of us don't financial plan:

1. **It's too confusing.**
2. **Bernie Madoff.**
3. **Procrastination**

Confusion

Reason #1 certainly makes sense; there is a lot of smoke and mirrors in the financial business. The media, Wall Street, bankers, CPA's, attorneys, *and* people like me are all to blame. We're living in the mega information era.

Last year one of my trusted wholesalers contacted me to schedule a breakfast and catch up on business. Mike worked for one of the largest insurance/investment companies in the world. He represented their Variable Annuity segment and was obsessed with providing the most current information regarding their products, the competition, and how it could all be used to better my clients. Mike was an Ace for my practice.

We got together at a 1950's themed diner on an early Thursday morning. After two bites of a delicious Western Omelet, the conversation quickly turned away from our usual economic updates and mathematical analysis. My friend and trusted associate had gone through a traumatic and close call with a brain operation a few weeks prior. Painful migraines had sadly proven itself to be a brain tumor.

He was his normal upbeat self, and proud to have pushed right through the operation and get back to his typical routine. After filling me in on this wild story, Mike looked at me as if making a guilty admission, "Listen bro, it's all the same."

"I'm sorry Mike, what's all the same?"

"Seriously who cares? We all market these different riders, step ups, death benefits, hedging strategies, and baffle em with bull crap. All I want is for people to save more." *If the top dogs of these financial products can't justify all these moving parts, how is the average investor going to differentiate?*

In 1993 The American Academy of Pediatrics estimated that young adults see 3,000 advertisements in a day... Radio ads, billboards, TV, placemats, and on and on[49]. That's before we even had internet and spam e-mail! So, how do we make a decision when they all seem so great? In psychology there is a term called "Channel Capacity". This is referring to how the

---

[49] "Ads Pollute Most Everything in Sight", Albuquerque Journal- June 27, 1993

brain can only retain so much information. Perhaps this is why doctors are so brilliant, but seemingly dumbfounded by finance.

I'm a perfect culprit myself. I've had countless stories from high school and college of memories that would last a lifetime... great accomplishments, endless nights with my best friends, getting lucky, and moments of laughter that made us cry and nearly piss our pants. If you asked me right now to share one, I'd probably be at a loss for words. However, when I hang out with my one buddy Mike, he could rattle them off all day. Once I hear it, it comes back to me as if it were yesterday. Perhaps this is my case of transacted memory. Having these special relationships allows us to expand our horizons without having to limit ourselves because we can depend on others via their memory.

So when our little brains are bombarded by so much, how do we make run of the mill decisions? Let's take it a step further, when we're besieged by complex gobbledygook promoted nonstop by financial institutions, where do we start?

Many of my clients say, "Hey I saw on CNBC, I read in Fortune magazine, or I heard on Bloomberg radio..." There are some brilliant thoughts on these publications, but ask yourself how do they stay in business? It's plain and simple, you're not paying an additional fee to hear Bloomberg or watch Fox, but every few minutes or pages they breakaway to sell us something. That's where they make their money, advertisers.

So how do they keep their financiers happy? Kissing their ass- If someone was paying you to stay alive, wouldn't you promote them versus the guys who give you jack? Plenty of first class publications list the "Top 10 Mutual Funds of the Year!", only to find in the following pages beautiful full page ads for each fund family. Mutual funds are a trillion dollar industry boosted by our own government, via the collapse of DB plans and installation of 401(k), IRA, 403(b) plans.

Hence remember the hidden motives. Did you know that NBC is owned by General Electric, ABC by Disney, CBS by Viacom, and CNN by AOL Time Warner? These are all publicly traded companies competing for a better stock price, via viewer ratings and advertiser dollars. They'll get there by any means necessary. They are also the main modes of communication to inform the decision making process.

Don't let yourself be overwhelmed. If I took you out to Ruth Chris and bought a big Filet Mignon, then shoved it down your throat; you'd choke and spit it all over me. But if you cut it up into little pieces, that steak would taste delightful. So slow down, do some research with real humans not the computer. As my friend Mike can help me remember all that I forget, a trusted Certified Financial Planner™ can allow you to focus elsewhere and then provide you that transacted memory when necessary.

Bernie Madoff

Reason #2 is also acceptable. Bernie Madoff is scum that should be stringed from light fixtures in front of the NYSE, medieval style. As the old saying goes, one rotten apple can spoil the bunch. I like to follow the Four-Way Test promoted by Rotary International. Because remember, good news travels fast, but bad news travels faster.

Hundreds of clients reject perfectly sound recommendations, because they've got a story. "Mutual Funds!? Those things are a racket... I know someone who."-

"Annuities!? You kidding me, my neighbor lost his shirt." "Life Insurance!? What a waste, I got wrapped into one of those things way back when." When people feel as if they've been burnt in the past, it automatically eliminates any future consideration. As if you had a bland pizza pie as a child and then refused to walk into an Italian restaurant the rest of your life. He who suffers remembers. A good story is worth more than the truth.

Needless to say, Wall Street, and all of finance for that matter, is not riding high right now. Joe the plumber does not see our crowd as a godsend. Capitalism is finance, and finance is math, and math does not have much in the way of sensitive attachment.

Your retail financial planner, people like me, are not at all like your institutional investor, the "Wall Street Guy". The only way we make a living is by getting referrals. And it's up to you to spread the word, if you like us, tell your friends, if we screw you, tell the papers. We don't get to hide for long.

Procrastination

Now Reason #3, that one chaps my ass. It really is the only one that we can't help you with, and you can't blame us for it. Many a false step was made by standing still.

Let me introduce you to Mr. and Mrs. NeedaFinancialPlan. I met them last April. They recently bought their first house, a beautiful new construction in a well to do neighborhood. They were both working in the city and making excellent incomes. Our discussion was provoked by the recent wonderful news, Mrs. NeedaFinancialPlan just found out she was pregnant, with twins!

I spoke with this lovely, young couple on the phone, "Bryan thank you so much for calling us. We feel like we're doing great in our careers, but frankly we don't know where the money goes. And now with kids on the way, we know we've got to get serious and plan for the future."

"Excellent, let's get started by scheduling an initial consultation," I reply.

"Well here's the thing," Mrs. Needafinancialplan begins, "It's April right now, and me and my husband are buried in work. In the afternoons and on Saturday and Sunday we like to go out to the park and enjoy the spring weather with the little bit of free time we do have."

"Well how about June then?"- "Well you see in June the summer is getting started, and that's our favorite time of the year. The kids are off from school, we plan a few vacations, and we love to get down to the beach with the little bit of free time that we do have."

"Jeez you folks are busy, well how is October then?"- "That would be perfect, except my husband is really into unwinding from the summer. When the leaves start to change and fall, it's beautiful. We like to sit on the back porch and soak it in with the little bit of free time that we do have."

"Well it looks like the only feasible time we'll have is in December then..."- "December!? Oh forget it, and then we have the holidays and all the snow to deal with. Winter is tough for us because we really hate going out in the cold, unless it's to ski or hike with the little bit of free time that we do have."

"Andddd April was?"- "That's when the sun breaks through and we love to go out and...."

Procrastination is the same excuse the fat guy on the couch uses. Don't pull that nonsense with your money. If at any point in the financial planning process it all becomes more important to ME than it does to YOU, we have a huge problem. A CFP® may be an incredibly knowledgeable co-pilot, but this is your plane!

There is never a perfect time to start planning, and there's always a great excuse to wait awhile. But that's how life passes us right by. We are called the human race, because we humans are always racing around. If prospective clients can't make time for a twenty minute conversation, they're going to need two hours.

The Millionaire Next Door was excellent in pointing out how high wealth accumulators spend a regular time every month to conduct planning (not trading or altering their portfolios) but analyzing their overall plans. The under wealth accumulators flat out did not plan, and the number one excuse was not enough time.

So those are the three big reasons why America sometimes sits still and poops its pants. If you've gotten past #1 and #2 (our fault) but are kind of stuck on #3 (your fault), remember that different isn't always better, but better is always different. Don't be so afraid of change or that second opinion. As the Buddhists say, "First intention, then enlightenment." Get motivated and make some decisions, like the luminary above says to. The decisions won't always be perfect, but that's ok, the journey never is, you'll correct course as you go.

Step 16: Everyone is a Salesman

"Do the thing you fear and death of fear is certain."
- Ralph Waldo Emerson

Sales invades every part of life. Whether it is wooing a girl on a date, convincing a teacher for a second chance, nailing the interview, landing the big promotion, garnering a vote, or acquiring a new customer. Like it or not, nothing happens until something is sold.

Great salesmen just have something in them, an aura that isn't turned off or on. I remember going out to lunch with one of the top pro's in our business. As part of the conversation I casually asked what's good here? He looked me in the eye and calmly described the succulent way they prepare their roasted duck and how it will melt in my mouth. I hate duck and the mere idea of eating one... That day I ate duck.

Business owners are fond of hiring their own version of a psychologist, or paid friend. We call it a business coach. My first coach upheld the creed "Be an ACE!" A- Active. C- Competitive. E- Efficient. The best in any industry make these 3 traits the foundation of their practice. Top agents are always on the go, want to be number one, and are unsparing with their time. They learn to be productive, not busy, living the doctrine that less isn't necessarily lazy.

Rookie salespeople should strive to "Score a Touchdown every day!" This is a Seven-Point sales system to track activity. One point equals fifteen phone calls, one point for a client/customer meeting, and one point for a qualified referral.

In my early days, I unfortunately didn't have a rolodex and client meetings were few and far between. You have to have clients in order to get referrals, so that left me to cold calling most days. I was determined to score my touchdown and as you guessed, that meant several days with 105 phone calls. Thomas Edison held that, "Genius is 1% inspiration, 99% perspiration."

Ray Kroc, the legendary founder of McDonald's was routinely cold called for various solicitations. Where most executives would tell their secretaries to play the role of gatekeeper and deny them, Kroc demanded that his secretaries "Send them all in". He firmly believed that courage was the most important trait in sales, and these guys were tough enough to find the courage to be judged solely on their own performance.

Cold calling is training camp. In football we spent countless hours lifting weights, running sprints, and watching film, but a tiny fraction of the time actually playing the game. If you took two equal athletes, but one spent the whole offseason busting his ass, and the other was chilling with his buddies, you could rest assured the trained brought a different kind of determination on game day. The lead up to customer interaction makes a salesperson appreciate and respect the opportunity.

The other beauty of cold calling is that the doldrums force a beginner to get creative and find new ways to prospect. Albert Einstein once said, "The monotony of a quiet life stimulates the creative mind." There is no lonelier moment than sitting in an empty cube room making dials to the sound of voicemails and clicks.

Take for instance one of the greatest scientific achievements in history, light. In an effort to obtain the contract to Manhattan's first power grid, Thomas Edison and Charles Brush were in a head to head competition. Edison fought to coax Manhattan's corrupt city government with a champagne dinner at Delmonico's. At the same time his opponent, Charles Brush, was doing a light display with arc light on Broadway. Edison successfully SOLD the politicians over dinner, and now he lives on in statues and TV shows while other inventors remain nameless.

Harry Overstredt said in *Influencing Human Behavior*, that "Action springs out of what we fundamentally desire... And the best piece of advice which can be given to would be persuaders, whether in business, home, school, politics is: First arouse in the other person an eager want. He who can do this has the whole world with him. He who cannot walks a lonely way." That final aim of personal connection defines sales.

What is the psychology behind arousing that "want"? Abe Lincoln once claimed, "If you want to win a man to your cause, first convince him that you are his friend." One of the most agreed upon steps to making an acquaintance a friend is to use their name (a civility we all too often forget). People exploit the easy copout of "I'm terrible with names", they're not terrible with names, they are just terrible. Addressing someone by name is a matter of concentration and self-abnegation. A person's name is the sweetest of sounds.

Sales training books expound that hominids have two ears and one mouth, use them proportionately. Ben Franklin famously said, "On Conversation- would you win the hearts of others, you must not seem to vie with them, but to admire them. Give them every opportunity of displaying their own qualifications, and when you have indulged their vanity, they will praise you in turn and prefer you above others... Such is the vanity of mankind what others say is a much surer way of pleasing than talking ourselves." You spend countless hours educating yourself to develop a unique skillset in your profession, bubbling at the brim to share this knowledge with prospects, but use caution to drop knowledge only when necessary. It was previously mentioned that a person's name is the sweetest of sounds; you might argue that their own voice is even sweeter!

In layman's terms, the sales conversation is akin to a dance or date. You move back and forth, feeling one another out, deciphering when to laugh and when to poke fun, smile, straighten up, flirt, mimic their movements, and so on. The successful salesman, or Don Juan with charm, controls this game. Reading different emotions is not always easy- Think about your favorite TV show from childhood up to adult comedy, the producers even have to insert crowd laughing or ominous music to let us audience know when it's ok to laugh or sob.

Conversely in scientific terms, the sales conversation is a chronicle with four ingredients. The Description- what is your service/product? The meaning- what does your service/product do? The Relevance- what does it do for YOU, the customer? The Value- what threat does it avoid, what obligation does it fulfill, or what opportunity does it exploit? These elements must be concisely explained, it's ok for a prospect to dislike you, but never let them misunderstand you. If your dance can't quickly display those necessities, you're going home alone.

Once you've listened to a client, utilize an acronym coined by the CIA's most secret spies. Moles are taught to "Remember the MICES". M- Money, I- Ideology, C- Compromise, E- Ego, and S- Sex. Spies believe that every man is susceptible to one of these four triggers; it is a salesperson's job to detect which one. This same psychology can be used to motivate a prospect to act in their own best interests and become a buyer. As Sun Tzu said in The Art of War, "To fight and conquer in all of your battles is not supreme excellence; supreme excellence consists in breaking the enemies resistance without fighting."

The quintessence of sales is the client experience. Everything can be bought readily on the internet without any human interaction, but employing the concepts mentioned above should ultimately create an experience that trumps the robotic approach. A perfect example of this is buying a coke at an amusement park. When the liter at Foodtown goes from $1.50 to $2 patrons are in an uproar. Yet we'll gladly pay about five times this at Six Flags without second thought. Why? Because humans value the unique experience in favor of convenience.

These occurrences that make up our days generate word of mouth, the single most important marketing plan today. Think about the last movie you saw, restaurant you ate at, hotel you visited... most of these adventures were probably recommended by a friend.

You must create a community around your friends, a center of influence, or sales force. It's like peer pressure that's getting everyone to move in the right action that you control.

Passionate groups can magnify an idea, regardless of its validity. The pyramid scheme leader epitomizes this.

The sales process should conclude with a close or in my industry a request for money. It's easy to fall prey to commission breath in the early years. So forget not this classic story...

The Steer and The Calf

There once was an old, wise steer and young, excited bull who sat together in the desert. Having been bored long enough, they decided to climb the highest mountain in the lands. Their trek began at sunup and didn't end until sunset. After an exhausting journey, they finally reached the peak. Both animals stared off into the distance at perfect vistas, full of pride. Then they gazed down into the valley and noticed hundreds of beautiful calf wading through the grass.

Out of breath the young bull quickly screamed, "Hey, what do you say we RUN down this mountain and tag us a calf!"

The old steer calmly looked over to him and slowly said, "Hey, how about we WALK down this mountain and tag em all."

Like the gentleman who sold me on the duck, sales is an appearance. It starts with the physical appearance which is controlled by emotions which are controlled by thoughts. In any interaction of business or situations that can lend themselves to business, be in complete control of thought... feel good, look good, and play good. In order await the disordered; in tranquility await the clamorous.

Lastly, for those of you on my side of the table, the tipping point moments are inevitable, "This deal is it! If I close it I'm going to be set, and if he says no, I'm outta here man." Do not jeopardize your own thoughts by what others might say or do. To save your sanity and pride, please define your sales, but never let them define you. I share with you a line from one of my favorite movies...

"Derice, a gold medal is a wonderful thing. But if you're not enough without one, you'll never be enough with one."- Irv Blitzer, coach of Jamaican Bobsled Team (Cool Runnings).

<u>Closing</u>

"Anything truly novel is invented only during one's youth.
Later one becomes more experienced, more
famous, and more blockheaded."
- Albert Einstein

    In the wake of the Cuban Missile Crisis, Richard and Robert Sherman wanted to convey a message of peace and brotherhood on earth. They wrote a song, originally as a ballad, and presented it to Walt Disney. Walt loved the song but found it to be too slow for any of his uses. Undeterred, the Sherman brothers picked up the tempo and sang in counterpoint. Walt fell in love and added the tune to one of his main attractions. Today it is arguably the most widely translated piece of music in history... "It's A Small World".

    We've all sung the song, and we've all had that feeling... it sure is a small world. It actually hasn't grown since the Great Depression, the Civil War, Revolutionary War, Dark Ages, Biblical times, and far before then. Matter of fact, this small world hasn't ever grown to our knowledge. But has it really always been this small? There is one more piece of data which reemphasizes why it is so crucial to be financially independent, because this small world isn't getting any bigger...

    If I tore this page in two and then placed the two halves on top of each other, and then repeated the process, the new thickness would be four times the original. If I repeated this process, say fifty times, how tall might it be? The geometric progress, Thickness x 2 to the 50th power, would create a stack of papers nearly reaching the sun.

The most common form of geometric progression is noticed in the human race. It took the earth's population thousands of years, from early mankind all the way until the 1800's to reach one billion people. Then astoundingly it took only 100 years (1920's) to reach two billion. Fast forward to 1970- four billion, today- nearly eight billion of us roam planet Earth! This progression of society creates rapid prosperity, interconnectedness, and inventions of all sorts at breakneck speed. Unfortunately it also creates the same multiplier effect on problems- terrorism, hunger, disease, debts, costs of living, etc.[50]

As the population propagates while the Earth's dimensions remain unchanged, we have an issue of apportioning significance to tasks at hand. A Granny Smith apple cut into eight slices sounds like a satisfying snack. Cut that same apple into 1,000 slices and good look finding a consumer. You are now one of those thousand slices, insignificant as an ant under the broad sky. However, no matter how you many times you keep slicing and dicing that apple, there will remain five carpels. Within those carpels are a set amount of seeds. Once that apple has seen its day, seeds will fall from the carpels and find a home in the earth. Out of that one apple will come hundreds, thousands, even millions of future apples. We each have a choice to be that tiny insignificant slice, or that seed that will feed generations to come.

We must not purge ourselves in the crowds. The statistics surrounding Social Security, Taxes, Healthcare Costs, College Education, Housing, Food, and Retirement Plans may be

---

[50] U.S. Census Bureau

overwhelming, but focusing on yourself and what you alone can do each day will foster financial freedom. Our generation's future and that of our unborn children will be dictated by these choices. Once you have mastered these sixteen steps, take advantage of exponential progression by teaching others. Therefore you will be a seed of the solution and not a slice of the problem. I wish you success as you implement these steps on your quest to become a millionaire by thirty!

Sincerely,

Bryan M. Kuderna, CFP®, LUTCF

This material contains the current opinions of Bryan Kuderna but not necessarily those of Guardian or its subsidiaries and such opinions are subject to change without notice.

Made in the USA
Columbia, SC
19 September 2019